# WHO IS
# JESUS CHRIST?

CHARLES HOLMES SR.

PAGE PUBLISHING, INC.
Conneaut Lake, PA

First originally published by Page Publishing 2020

ISBN 978-1-6624-1505-0 (pbk)
ISBN 978-1-6624-1506-7 (digital)

Printed in the United States of America

# Preface

Who is Jesus Christ?

Is Jesus just a man? Is Jesus just a prophet? Is Jesus just a preacher? Is Jesus a religious leader? When reading this book, we will discover that Jesus is more than a religious leader. Because religion cannot save you. You cannot go to heaven through religion, you must go through Jesus. Jesus is 100 percent man and 100 percent God in the flesh. Jesus is Lord, Jesus is God, Jesus is the savior of the world. Jesus is the redeemer. Jesus atone for our sin on the cross. Jesus is our righteousness, Jesus is our justifier, is our sanctifier, Jesus is our advocate, Jesus is our mediator, Jesus is our victory over death, hell, and the grave. Jesus is our righteous judge. Without Jesus, we cannot worship God. Jesus is the highway to heaven, the Bible is the road map.

# Jesus Is Our Lord and Savior

Savior means one who brings salvation. And Jesus brings salvation because he is the savior of the world. He is not just the savior of the United States. But of the world. The Word of God says, "That God so love the world that he gave is only begotten son, that whosoever believeth in him, should not perish but have everlasting life."

There is only one savior of the world, Jesus Christ, the righteous. There are many religion and many religious leaders but only one Lord and savior. There is only one redeemer. Redeemer means one who save others from distress and is the messianic title for Jesus. In order for your sins to be blotted out, you must have a redeemer to redeem you back to God. Because the redeemer dies for your sins. The redeemer must give his life in order to save your life. He is the savior of the world, and the redeemer must die for the sins of the world. The Word of God says, "For the wages of sin is death but the gift of God is eternal life through Jesus Christ our Lord" (Romans 6:23).

Salvation is a gift; you don't have to work for it. "For God so loved the world that he gave his only begotten son, that whosoever believeth in him should not perish, but have everlasting life" (John 3:16). So you have a choice, eternal life or eternal death. Religion cannot forgive or wash away sin, neither work can. Without the shedding of blood, there is no remising of sin, forgiveness of sin (Hebrews 9:22). You cannot work off sin that must be atone for. Atone means reconciliation of God and man through Christ's sacrificial death on the cross.

"On the day of atonement, the high priest would make an atonement for the people's sins once a year, with two goats and a bullock, then he shall kill the goat of the sin offering, that is for the people, and bring his blood within the veil and do with that blood as he did with the blood of the bullock and sprinkle it upon the mercy seat. And he shall make an atonement for the holy place because of the uncleanness of the children of Israel and because of their transgressions in all their sins: and so shall he do for the tabernacle of the congregation, that remaineth among them in the midst of their uncleanness. And there shall be no man in the tabernacle of the congregation when he goeth in to make an atonement in the holy place until he come out and have made an atonement for himself, and for his household, and for all the congregation of Israel. And he shall go out unto the altar that is before the Lord and make an atonement for it and shall take of the blood of the bullock, and of the blood of the goat, and put it upon the horns of the altar round about. And he shall sprinkle of the blood upon it with his finger seven times and cleanse it, and hallow it from the uncleanness of the children of Israel. And when he hath made an end of reconciling the holy place and the tabernacle of the congregation and the altar, he shall bring the live goat. And Aaron shall lay both his hands upon the head of the live goat and confess over him all the iniquities of the children of Israel and all their transgressions in all their sins putting them upon the head of the goat, and shall send him away by the hand of a fit man into the wilderness. And the goat shall bear upon him all their iniquities unto a land not inhabited, and he shall let go the goat in the wilderness" (Leviticus 16:15–22).

The blood of bullock and goats atone for our sins, then God forgives it. Jesus atone for our sins on the cross by shedding his blood, then God forgives it. Without the shedding of blood, there is no forgiveness of your sins. In the Old Testament, the people had a high priest which made an atonement for the people of God once a year. In the New Testament, Jesus Christ is our high priest, which atone for our sins once and for all. "But Christ being come an high priest of good things to come, by a greater and more perfect tabernacle, not made with hands, that is to say, not of this building. Neither by blood of goats and calves but by his own blood, he entered in once into the holy place, having obtained eternal redemption for us. For if the blood of bulls and of goats and the ashes of an heifer sprinkling the unclean, sanctifieth to the purifying of the flesh, how much more shall the blood of Christ, who through the eternal spirit offered himself without spot to God, purge your conscience from dead works to serve the living God?" (Hebrews 9:11–14)

Jesus gave his life for us on the cross. He was buried for three days then resurrected from the dead. He went to heaven into the holy of the holy, not made with hands, and he place his blood on the mercy seat in heaven to atone for the sins of the whole world, once and for all. That is why Jesus died on the cross and said it is finish, it is finish! Our salvation has been purchase by the blood of Jesus. No religious leader can say that because they must be redeemed. No religion can save you but Christianity or forgive your sin but God. God forgives your sin, and the blood of Jesus cleanses you from your sins. God cannot forgive your sins except through the blood of Jesus. No denomination can save you, no preacher can save you, no religious leader can save you, and water cannot save you, nothing but the blood of Jesus. Because the redeemer must die, water cannot die, religion cannot die, the redeemer must give his life so I may have eternal life. The redeemer must be a man, the redeemer must be holy and without sin. The only man that is holy without sin is God, so only God can redeem us.

God came in sinful flesh, in a form of a man, to redeem us from our sin. "Wherefore, as by one (Adam) sin entered into the world, and death by sin; and so death passed upon all men, for that all have sinned" (Romans 5:12). Sin had entered the world by a man, so it took a man to redeem us from our sin. For it is not possible that the blood of bulls and of goats should take away sins. "Wherefore when he came into the world, he saith, 'Sacrifice and offering thus wouldest not, but a body hast thou prepared me; in burnt offering and sacrifices for sin thou had no pleasure.' Then said I, 'Lord, I come in the volume of the book, it is written of me to do thy will of God'" (Hebrews 10:4–7). The blood of bulls and goats could never take away your sin, it just covers your sins. It took Jesus Christ to take away your sins, so God gave him a body to redeem the whole world. "And by the which will we are sanctified through the offering of the body of Jesus Christ once for all" (Hebrews 10:10).

Until you are born again, you are spiritually dead. Death mean separation when you are naturally dead, that means souls are separated from your body. When you are spiritually dead, that means your soul is separated from God. If you are a sinner or religious, you are separated from God, and you have to be born again. Because you are spiritually dead, that means you are in your sins, for the wages of sin is death but the gift of God is eternal life. "Behold the Lord's hand is not shortened that it cannot save; neither his ear heavy that it cannot hear: But your iniquities have separated between you and your God, and your sin have hidden his face from you that he will not hear" (Isaiah 59:1–2).

When you are birthed into this world, this is born of the flesh. That is the natural birth, we are born spiritually dead because we inherit a sin nature from Adam. When you are born again, that is the spiritual birth, which is the second birth. Your sin is forgiven by God, the blood of Jesus cleanses you, and the Holy Spirit quickens your spirit, which is call regeneration, that is called the new birth in the believer. "Not by works of righteousness which we have done but according to his mercy he saved us by the washing of regeneration and renewing of the Holy Ghost, which he shed on us abundantly through Jesus Christ our Savior; that being justified by his grace, we should be made heirs according to the hope of eternal life" (Titus 3:5–7).

"And you hath he quickened, who were dead in trespasses and sins" (Ephesians 2:1). For we are save through the grace of God, not through religion or works of righteousness but through the finish work of Jesus on the cross by redeeming us. "For by grace are ye saved through faith; and that not of yourselves: it is the gift of God, not of works lest any man should boast" (Ephesians 2:8–9).

"That if thou shalt confess with thy mouth, the Lord Jesus, and shalt believeth in thine heart that God hath raised him from the dead, thou shalt be saved. For with the heart, man believeth unto righteousness, and with the mouth confession is made unto salvation" (Romans 10:9–10).

# Redemption, Justification, Righteousness

When we are redeemed through the sacrifice death of Jesus on the cross, we are justified and declared righteous before God. What is redemption? Salvation is accomplished by someone paying the price for sin. What is righteousness? It inherent or imputed and guiltlessness before God. What is justification? God accounting the guilty to be righteous and acceptable because of Christ's death. Once saved, you have been delivered from the power of sin. That does not mean that you want sin, that just mean you are no longer in bondage to sin. When a Christian sin, he sins because he is tempted and because he is walking in the flesh and not walking in the spirit, but he is still a Christian. All he have to do is repent and ask forgiveness for his sins through Jesus's name, and God will forgive him. But when a sinner sins, he sins by nature which he received through Adam. You can go to church seven days a week and eight times on Sunday, and you will still die in your sins. Accept that you will be saved through Jesus Christ.

When Jesus Christ comes back for the church, he is not coming back for a building, he is coming back for a spiritual church, which is a body of believer in Jesus Christ. "And he is the head of the body, the church who is the beginning the firstborn from the dead, that in all things he might have the preeminence" (Colossians 1:18). "There is only one church, and to be in this church, you must be redeemed by the blood of the Lamb of God which taketh away the sin of the world. Who hath delivered us from the power of darkness and hath translated us into the kingdom (the spiritual church) of his dear son; in whom we have redemption through his blood, even the forgiveness of sins; who is the image of the invisible God, the firstborn of every creature" (Colossians 1:13–15). Because the church is blood bought and purchased by the blood of Jesus Christ.

"Take heed therefore unto yourselves and to all the flock over the which the Holy Ghost hath made you overseers, to feed the Church of God, which he hath purchased with his own blood" (Acts 20:28). "To wit, that God was in Christ, reconciling the world unto himself, not imputing their trespasses unto them; and hath committed unto us the word of reconciliation" (2 Corinthians 5:19). Because our sins have separated us from God, and we needed a sin bearer to reconcile us back to God. What is a sin bearer? One who takes the sins of another upon himself. Jesus is our scapegoat because he bore all our sins. The scapegoat must be innocent, that means free from sin, free from guilt or blame, free from evil influence or effect. "For he (God) hath made him (Jesus) to be sin for us, who knew no sin; that we might be made the righteousness of God in him" (2 Corinthians 5:21). None but the righteous shall see God. Church attendance will not make you righteous or save you.

Church denomination will not make you righteous or save you. Religion of any kind will make you righteous, redeem you, or justify your sin. Nothing but the blood of Jesus can wash away your sins. "Therefore, by the deeds (works) of the law, there shall no flesh be justified in his sight for by the law is the knowledge of sin. But now the righteousness of God (Jesus) without the law is manifested, being witnessed by the law and the prophets even the righteousness of God which is by faith of Jesus Christ unto all and upon all them that believe. For there is no difference for all have sinned and come short of the glory of God. Being justified freely by his grace through the redemption that is in Christs Jesus whom God hath set forth to be a propitiation through faith in his blood to declare his righteousness for the remission (forgiveness) of sins that are passed through the forbearance of God. To declare, I say, at this time his righteousness that he might be just and the justifier of him which believeth in Jesus" (Romans 3:20–26).

To be righteous under the law, we would have to keep the whole law, which could not because of the weakness of the flesh. We could not work, do good deeds to be righteous, or redeemed ourselves because work and deeds cannot forgive sin. Only God can forgive sin through Jesus Christ. Because someone has to atone for your sins, and that someone must die. Jesus is that someone. "Therefore, being justified by faith, we have peace with God through our Lord Jesus Christ by whom also we have access by faith into this grace wherein we stand and rejoice in hope of the glory of God" (Romans 5:1–2).

"But God commendeth his love toward us in that while we were yet sinners, Christ died for us. Much more then, being now justified by his blood, we shall be saved from wrath through him. For if, when we were enemies, we were reconciled to God by the death of his son, much more, being reconciled, we shall be saved by his life. And not only so, but we also joy in God through our Lord Jesus Christ by whom we have now received the atonement" (Romans 5:8–11).

You either have been justified or you are condemned. If you are saved, then you have been justified; if you are a sinner, then you are condemned. Condemned means you are guilty before God of your sins. You are either saved or lost, righteous or unrighteous, justified or condemned. Remember, no religion justifies you because you cannot work off sin, it must be atoned for. "Therefore, as by the offence of one (Adam), judgment came upon all men to condemnation. Even so by the righteousness of one (Jesus), the free gift came upon all men unto justification of life. For as by one man's (Adam) disobedience, many were made sinners, so by the obedience of one (Jesus) shall many be made righteous" (Romans 5:18–19).

Only Jesus Christ can justify your sin. You cannot justify your sins, neither water can justify them. You must be born again. Until you are born again, you are spiritually dead and still in your sins. "And he spake this parable unto certain which trusted in themselves that they were righteous and despised others. Two men went up into the temple to pray, the one a Pharisee and the other a publican. The Pharisee stood and prayed thus with himself, 'God, I thank thee that I am not as other men are, extortioner unjust, adulterers, or even as this publican. I fast twice in the week, I give tithes of all that I possess.' And the publican, standing a far off, would not lift up so much as his eyes unto heaven but smote upon his breast, saying, 'God, be merciful to me, a sinner.' I tell you, this man went down to his house justified rather than the other for every one that exalteth himself shall be abased, and he that humbleth himself shall be exalted. The Pharisee trusted in himself that he was righteous, that is called self-righteousness" (Luke 18:9–14).

Because he thinks he is righteous base upon works of righteousness, but the publican asked God to have mercy upon him, and he was justified. That is what God wants us to do, to ask for mercy, repent of our, and be saved. "For I say unto you, 'That except your righteousness shall exceed the righteousness of the scribes, and, Pharisees, ye shall in no case enter into the kingdom of heaven" (Matthew 5:20). Righteousness, which is religious, want to get you into heaven, but that exceeding righteousness is faith in Jesus Christ, not self or religion. "And it came to pass as Jesus sat at meat in the house. Behold, many publicans and sinners come and sat down with him and his disciples. And when the Pharisees saw it, they said unto his disciples, 'Why eateth your master with publicans and sinners?' But when Jesus heard that, he said unto them, 'They that be whole need not a physician, but they that are sick. But go ye and learn what that meaneth, I will have mercy, not sacrifice for I am not come to call the righteous but sinners to repentance'" (Matthew 9:10–13).

Jesus did not come the righteous but sinners to repent, so the Pharisee had to repent as well as the publicans and sinners because they were not righteous, either because religion cannot make you righteous. No matter what religion you are a part of, you are still a sinner. Only faith in Jesus can make you righteous. "Because none is righteous, no not one, we all come short of the glory of God. But we are all as an unclean thing, and all our righteousness are as filthy rags, and we all do fade as a leaf and our iniquities, like the wind have taken us away" (Isaiah 64:6). That mean the best that we can do for righteousness before God is unclean, filthy, not good enough, and is rejected by God because effort is not good enough. You are condemned or justified no in between. In whom we have redemption through his blood, the forgiveness of sins, according to the riches of his grace.

# Jesus Is the Gospel

What is the gospel? The gospel is the death, burial, and resurrection of Jesus Christ. The gospel is Jesus and Jesus is the gospel. You cannot separate the two because they are one. "In whom ye also trusted after that ye heard the word of truth, the gospel of your salvation. In whom also after that ye believed, ye were sealed with that Holy Spirit of promise" (Ephesians 1:13).

By his death on the cross, he saved us. By his burial, he carried our sins far away. By his resurrection, he justified us and freed us forever. You have two church, the true church and the false church. To be in the true church, you must believe the gospel; the true church is the body of believers. The true church is the body of Jesus Christ, not a building. After believing the gospel, you are baptized into the body of Christ by the Holy Spirit. "For as the body is one and hath many members, and all the members of that one body, being many, are one body, so also is Christ. For by one spirit are we all baptized into one body, whether we be bond or free and have been all made to drink into one spirit. For the body is not one member but many" (1 Corinthians 12:12–14).

There is only one true church, the body of believer. One true God, one Savior, and only way to heaven, believe the gospel of Jesus Christ. "Jesus said unto him, 'I am the way, the truth, and the life, no man cometh unto the father, but by me'" (John 14:6). Jesus is the way, not a way. So that canceled out all religion but Christianity. No religion can get you to heaven, neither works or good deeds can get you to heaven no matter how great they're may be. Because religion or works cannot take away sins, you need a sin bearer, Jesus Christ. There is only one true gospel, and that is the gospel of Jesus Christ. There are only four gospel books and four gospel writers, Matthew, Mark, Luke, and John. You have heard about the gospel of Judas, the gospel of Thomas, the gospel of Mary Magdalene, and to make these book believable, you have the so-called gospel of Peter.

These books are not the gospel of Jesus Christ. What is the gospel of Jesus Christ? The gospel of Jesus Christ is the death, burial, and resurrection of Jesus Christ, that's the gospel of Jesus Christ, the true gospel. And if these books do not have the death, burial, and resurrection of Jesus Christ, then it is not the true gospel of Jesus Christ. The gospel of Jesus Christ is not a novel or some history book. It is the Word of God. The true gospel does not talk about performing magic or glay pigeon and Jesus being married to Mary Magdalene and they having children. "For we are the children of God by faith in Christ Jesus" (Galatians 3:28). The gospel of Jesus Christ brings salvation. There is no salvation in these so-called books of the gospel. Neither God nor Jesus perform magic; Jesus performs miracles. There is no salvation in magic and glay pigeon, only in the gospel. The bishops of the early church did not accept these books as the true gospel of Jesus Christ. The gospel of Matthew, Mark, Luke, and John talk about the death, burial, and resurrection of Jesus Christ and salvation and the miracles that Jesus performed. "For the son of man has come to save that which was lost" (Matthew 18:11 and Luke 19:10).

"Jesus said unto her, 'I am the resurrection and life. He that believeth in me, though he were dead, yet shall he live, and whosoever liveth and believeth in me shall never die. Believest thou this?' She saith unto him, 'Yea, Lord. I believe that thou art the Christ, the son of God which should come into the world'" (John 11:25–27). Now after that, John was put in prison.

"Jesus came into Galilee, preaching the gospel of the kingdom of God and saying, 'The time is fulfilled, and the kingdom of God is at hand. Repent ye and believe the gospel'" (Mark 1:14–15). The gospel of Jesus Christ saves those that believe the gospel. If the gospel cannot save, then it is not the gospel. When Jesus commission his apostle, he said in the gospel of Matthew. "And Jesus came and spake unto them, saying, 'All power is given unto me in heaven and in earth. Go ye therefore and teach all nations, baptizing them in the name of the Father and of the Son and of the Holy Ghost. Teaching them to observe all things whatsoever I command you, and lo I am with you always even unto the end of the world. Amen'" (Matthew 28:18–20) And the gospel of Mark says, "He that believeth and is baptized shall be save, but he that believeth not shall be damned" (Mark 16:16). And the gospel of Luke says, "And said unto them, 'Thus it is written and thus it be hooved Christ to suffer and to rise from the dead the third day. And that repentance and remission of sins should be preached in his name among all nations, beginning at Jerusalem. And ye are witnesses of these things" (Luke 24:46–48).

And in the book of Acts, the apostles bear witness that Jesus Christ is Lord and savior of the world. And what did they preach? The gospel of Jesus Christ. And what did Apostle Paul preached in his epistles? The gospel of Jesus Christ. If the so-called gospel does not redeem or justifies you or declare you righteous, then it is a false gospel. Paul preached on false gospel in the book of Galatians. "'I marvel that ye are so soon removed from him that called you into the grace of Christ unto another gospel, which is not another but there be some that trouble you and would pervert the gospel of Christ. But though we, or an angel from heaven, preach any other gospel unto you than that which we have preached unto you, let him be accursed.' As we said before, so say I now again, 'If any man preach any other gospel unto you than that ye have received, let him be accursed for do I now persuade men or God? Or do I seek to please men? For if I yet please men, I should not be the servant of Christ. But I certify you, brethren, that the gospel which was preached of me is not after man. For I neither received it of man, neither was I taught it, but by the revelation of Jesus Christ'" (Galatians 1:6–12).

Paul is saying, if any false prophet or preacher preach any other gospel to you other than the gospel of Jesus Christ, let him be accurse or let him be damned. Satan have a false church, a false gospel, false prophets, and a false way to go to heaven. Satan have many religions to confuse you so you would not know what to believe. Satan not only tries to deceive sinners but he also tries to deceive believers of Jesus Christ. "For I am jealous over you with godly jealousy, for I have espoused you to one husband that I may present you as a chaste virgin to Christ. But I fear, lest by any means, as the serpent beguiled (trick) Eve through his subtlety (craftiness) so your minds should be corrupted from the simplicity (purity) that is in Christ. For if he that cometh preacheth another Jesus, whom we have not preached, or if ye receive another spirit, which ye have not received or another gospel, which ye have not received or another gospel, which ye have not accepted, ye might well bear with him" (2 Corinthians 11:2–4).

When we are born again through believing of the gospel of Jesus Christ, we are married to Jesus by salvation in his blood. We are the bride, the church, the body of believer, and Jesus is the bridegroom. Christianity is more than religion, it is a relationship with God through Jesus Christ. You must be born again or be lost. The Apostle Paul said this, "Moreover, brethren, I declare unto you the gospel which I preached unto you, which also ye have received and where in ye stand, by which also ye are saved if ye keep in memory what I preach unto you unless ye have believed in vain. For I delivered unto you first of all that which I also received, how that Christ died for our sins according to the scriptures. And that he was buried and that he rose again the third day according to the scriptures. And that he was seen of Ceplias (Peter) then of the twelve. After that, he was seen of above five hundred brethren at once of whom the greater part remain unto this present but some are fallen asleep" (1 Corinthians 15:1–6).

Satan attacks the gospel of Jesus Christ because the Christians faith hinges and is based on the gospel of Jesus Christ, which is the death, burial, and resurrection of Jesus Christ. By his death, he saved us, by his burial, he carried our sin far away, and by his resurrection, he justified us. When he died on the cross, he died sinless and holy. When he was buried, he was buried sinless and holy. If he had died in sin, he could not get up. A sinner cannot redeem sinner; the redeemer must be sinless and holy. He could not have ever sinned. The only person that have never is God, which is our redeemer through Jesus Christ, our Savior and Lord.

"Now, if Christ be preached that he rose from the dead, how say some among you that there is no resurrection of the dead? But if there be no resurrection of the dead, then is Christ not risen? And if Christ be not risen, then is our preaching vain and your faith is also vain? Yea, and we are found false witnesses of God because we have testified of God that he raised up Christ whom he raised not up, if so be that the dead rise not. For if the dead rise not, then is not Christ raised. And if Christ be not raised, your faith is vain. Ye are yet in your sins. Then they also which are fallen asleep in Christ are perished. If in this life only we have hope in Christ, we are of all men most miserable. But now is Christ risen from the dead and become the first fruits of them that slept. For since by man (Adam) came death, by man (Christ) came also the resurrection of the dead. For as in Adam all die, even so in Christ shall all be made alive" (I Corinthians 15:12–22).

Religion is the only hope you have in this life, which is false. Because when you die, you die with no hope of eternal life, you will die lost. But in Jesus Christ, we die with the hope of eternal life, will be with God for all eternity. When a Christian dies in Jesus Christ, we die saved. But when a religious person dies in their religion, they die lost and in their sins. "But us also to whom it shall be imputed, if we believe on him that raised up Jesus our Lord from the dead who was delivered for our offences (sins) and was raised again for our justification" (Romans 4:24–25).

Satan attacks the gospel of Jesus Christ because the gospel of Jesus Christ is the core and foundation of Christianity. Without the gospel of Jesus Christ, there is no Christianity. So, Satan try to pervert the true gospel by the false gospel, which cannot save. Only the true gospel can save; the purpose of the gospel is to save. Christianity is the only religion that Satan attacks, and the reason he attacks Christianity is because he knows that Christianity is the real thing. There is only one God, one redeemer, one church, one way to God, and one way to heaven. Remember, Jesus is the savior of the world, not just the United States of America, for the whole world. Satan try to make you think you can go to heaven by any religion or by works of righteousness, but you cannot. Jesus said, "I am the way, not a way." "But if our gospel be hid, it is hid to them that are lost. In whom the god of this world hath blinded the mind of them that believe not, lest the light of the glorious gospel of Christ, who is the image of God, should shine unto them. For we preach not ourselves but Christ Jesus, the Lord, and ourselves, your servants, for Jesus's sake" (II Corinthians 4:3–5).

If a preacher is a true man of God, he is going to preach the gospel of Jesus Christ. Jesus must be the center of the church, not self, because Jesus is the church. Jesus died for the church, not for a motivational speech or message or motivational speaker. We have a lot of motivation and no salvation, justification, and no sanctification in the church and repenting of our sins. The Bible says in the latter days that some will have itching ears. Itching ears is when a preacher preaches what you want to hear. He preaches a feel-good gospel or a feel-good message. We must preach the true gospel of Jesus Christ. "The Lord is not slack concerning his promise, as some men count concerning his promise, as some men count slackness but is long-suffering to us, ward not willing that any should perish but that all should come to repentance" (2 Peter 3:9). "And this gospel of the kingdom shall be preached in all the world for a witness unto all nations and then shall the end come" (Matthew 24:14).

The gospel shall be preached to all nations, not some nation because the gospel of Jesus Christ is the Word of God, which bring salvation unto all men who believe the gospel. "But we speak the wisdom of God in a mystery even the hidden wisdom, which God ordained before the world unto our glory. Which none of the princes (demons, Satan) of this world knew for had they known it, they would not have crucified the Lord of glory" (I Corinthians 2:7–8). Jesus was preordained to die for the sin of the world before the foundation of the world. Satan thought that by crucifying Jesus, he would stop God's plan of salvation for the world, but he did just what God wanted him to do. Because the wisdom of God is much higher than man. And his ways are pass finding out. Nothing can redeem you but blood of Jesus; no religion can redeem you but one, Christianity. To go to heaven, you must be redeemed from your sins.

"For as much as ye know that ye were not redeemed with corruptible things, as silver and gold, from your vain conversation received by tradition from your fathers but with the precious blood of Christ, as a lamb without blemish and without spot who verily was foreordained before the foundation of the world, but was manifest in these last times for you, who by him do believe in God, that raised him up from the dead and gave him glory; that your faith and hope might be in God. Seeing ye have purified your souls in obeying the truth through the spirit unto unfeigned love of the brethren, see that ye love one another with a pure heart fervently being born again, not of corruptible seed but of incorruptible, by the Word of God, which liveth and abideth forever. For all flesh is as grass, and all the glory of man as the flower of grass. The grass withereth and the flower thereof falleth away, but the word of the Lord endureth forever. And this is the word which by the gospel is preached unto you" (1 Peter 1:18–25).

If the so-called gospel of Judas, Thomas, and Mary Magdalene do not have these kinds of words in it, then it is not the gospel of Jesus Christ because the gospel saves. Because the gospel of Jesus Christ is the death, burial, and resurrection of Jesus, not magic, glay pigeon, or of any private interpretation to Mary Magdalene and not to Peter. "Knowing this first that no prophecy of the scripture is of any private interpretation for the prophecy came not in old time by the will of man but holy men of God spake as they were moved by the Holy Ghost" (2 Peter 1:20–21).

When a preacher is called into the ministry, he is called to preach the gospel of Jesus Christ. Even the Lord Jesus Christ preached the gospel, and he is the gospel. "For Christ sent me not to baptize but to preach the gospel not with wisdom of words, lest the cross of Christ should be made of none effect. For the preaching of the cross is to them that perish foolishness but unto us which are saved it is the power of God" (1 Corinthians 1:17–18). Paul is not saying that you should not be baptized, he is saying that baptism alone will not save anyone, you must believe and be baptized.

"And he said unto them, 'Go ye into all the world and preach the gospel to every creature. He that believeth and is baptize shall be saved, but he that believeth not shall be damned'" (Mark 16:15–16). Water cannot take away your sins, religion cannot take away your sins, and denomination cannot take away your sins. The redeemer must die so you can have life eternal; he must shed his blood for your sins. Satan had us bound by sins, living in sin, and spiritually blind, living in darkness. Then Jesus came and set us free from the power of the devil. And Jesus said this, "The Spirit of the Lord is upon me, because he hath anointed me to preach the gospel to the poor; he hath sent me to heal the broken hearted, to preach deliverance to the captives, and recovering of sight to the blind, to set at liberty them that are bruised, to preach the acceptable year of the Lord" (Luke 4:18–19 and Isaiah 61:1–2).

The savior and redeemer have come into the world to save that which was lost. "For I am not ashamed of the gospel of Christ for it is the power of God unto salvation to everyone that believed to the Jew first and also to the Greek (Gentile)" (Romans 1:16). Salvation is confession of your faith in Jesus Christ. You must believe that he died on the cross for your sin, and you cannot be ashamed of your Lord and Savior. He said, "If you are ashamed of me, then I will be ashamed of you before God and the holy angel, which is in heaven. Salvation is an open confession to God and the holy angel. "That if thou shalt confess with thy mouth the Lord Jesus and shalt believe in thine heart that God hath raised him from the dead, thou shalt be saved. For with the heart, man believeth unto righteousness and with the mouth confession is made unto salvation" (Romans 10:9–10).

# Jesus Is God in the Flesh

When you say Jesus is Lord, you are saying Jesus is God in the flesh. "There is one body (church) and one Spirit, even as ye are called in one hope of your calling; one Lord, one faith, one baptism, one God and Father of all, who is above all and though all and in you all" Ephesians 4:4–6. There is only one church, the Christian church; there is only one Lord, Jesus Christ; there is only one faith in God, that is Christianity; and there is only one God. This God have made heaven and earth and every human being. So, where all these God came from, there is only one God, not many, there is only one way to heaven, not many.

"Remember the former things of old: for I am God and there is none else. I am God, and there is none like me. Declaring the end from the beginning, and from ancient times the things that are not yet done, saying, my counsel (word) shall stand, and I will do all my pleasure" (Isaiah 46:9–10). When you can declare the end of the world from the beginning, you are God. When you can say how it going to end, you are God. And no king, prime minister, president, or man or woman can change it, you are God. If your god cannot do these things, then he is not God. There is nothing too hard for God. Can your god create the heavens and earth? "The earth is the Lord's, and the fullness thereof, the world, and they that dwell therein. For he hath founded it upon the seas and established it upon the floods. Who shall ascend into the hill of the Lord? Or who shall stand in his holy place? He that hath clean hands and a pure heart. Who hath not lifted up his soul unto vanity nor sworn deceitfully. He shall receive the blessing from the Lord and righteousness from the God of his salvation" (Psalm 24:1–5).

The God that we serve through Jesus Christ is the God of Abraham, Isaac, and Jacob, and beside him, there is no other God. "For there are three that bear record in heaven, the Father, the Word

(Son), and the Holy Ghost, and these three are one. (1 John 5:7). God is three in one, God the Father, God the Son, and God the Holy Ghost. God our Father, God our savior, and God our comforter and keep. Just like we are body, spirit, and soul. The soul is the will, mind, and emotion; the spirit is the heart, conscience, that lives in our body. We are three in one body. The word is the son made flesh. "And the word was made flesh, and dwelt among us (and we beheld his glory, the glory as of the only begotten of the father), full of grace and truth" (John 1:14). God and Christ are one, they operate separately, but they equal in power. God is our heavenly Father, Christ is the son and redeemer, and the Holy Ghost is our comforter.

When Christ said he is the son of God, he is saying that he is God in flesh. The Pharisees did not understand that they knew that God is a spirit, and Jesus is flesh and blood. "To wit, that God was in Christ, reconciling the world unto himself, not imputing their trespasses unto them and hath committed unto us the word of reconciliation" (2 Corinthians 5:19). The Pharisees knew that God is one, there is not two, three, or many God, they knew that there is only one true living God. And Jesus is flesh and blood. "I and my Father are one. Then the Jews took up stones again to stone him. Jesus answered them, 'Many good works have I shown you from my Father, for which of these works do ye stone me?' The Jews answered him, saying, 'For a good work we stone thee not but for blasphemy and because that thou, being a man, makest thyself God'" (John 10:30–33).

"Hear o Israel, the Lord our God is one God and thou shalt love the Lord thy God with all thine heart and with all thy soul and with all thy might" (Deuteronomy 6:4–5). So, they accused him of blasphemy, and blasphemy is punishable by death. Either Jesus is God in the flesh or he is a liar, and no liar can redeem the world. He would have to be redeemed, but Jesus never ask for forgiveness. Because he is Lord and God in the flesh. It was part of Satan's plan to have him stone; if he hadn't been stoned and crucified on the cross, we could not have been redeemed. "And he that blasphemeth the name of the Lord, he shall surely be put to death, and all the congregation shall certainly stone him as well the stranger (Gentik ) as he that is born in the land, when he blasphemeth the name of the Lord, shall be put to death" (Leviticus 24:16).

Jesus had to have been God in the flesh or we have two Lords. There is only one Lord, one faith, one baptism, one God, and one Father. When the Israelite enter the promise land, Moses reminded them that the Lord our God is one God. And that they should not worship any false god, idol god, or any false deity. "For the Lord your God is God of gods, and Lord of lords, a great God, a mighty, and a terrible, which regardeth not persons nor taketh reward" (Deuteronomy 10:17). I saw a woman on television, who said, "Jesus came to earth to make himself king, but he failed. Because he was crucified on the cross." "Therefore, doth my Father love me because I lay down my life that I might take it again. No man taketh from me, but I lay it down of myself. I have power to lay it down, and I have power to take it again. This commandment have I received of my Father" (John 10:17–18).

Nobody took Jesus's life, he laid it down for the sins of the world and took it up by rising on the third day. And by his death, he redeemed us and freed us forever that believe the gospel. "And a superscription also was written over him in letters of Greek and Latin and Hebrew, 'This is the king of the Jews'" (Luke 23:38). Not only is he king of the Jews, he is King of kings, and Lord of lords. He is King of the Jews because he is the son of David through the lineage of David by the tribe of Juda. He is the Lord of lords by the resurrection from the dead.

"Concerning his Son, Jesus Christ our Lord, which was made of the seed of David according to the flesh and declared to be the Son of God with power according to the spirit of holiness by the resurrection from the dead" (Romans 1:3–4). "And thine house and thy kingdom shall be established forever" (2 Samuel 7:16). David, the second king of Israel, came from the tribe of Juda, and King Jesus came from the tribe of Juda. He is king of the Jews and King of kings because Jesus is alive and well, because Jesus is the son of David according to the flesh, and the last king of Israel. When you can get up from the grave and rise from the dead, you are Lord. Jesus is the only one that got from the dead who said that he was sent by

God. "If you cannot get up from the dead, then you are nor Lord or the Son of God. And he hath on his vesture and on his thigh a name written, 'King of kings, and Lord of lords'" (Revelation 19:16). The Word of God has prophesied of the coming of Jesus Christ as savior, redeemer, the Messiah and prophet. But the Word of God has no record of these so-called savior, false Messiah, false prophet, and religious leaders. But the Word of God speaks for Jesus. "I will raise them up a prophet from among their brethren, like unto thee and will put my words in his mouth, and he shall speak unto them all that I shall command him" (Deuteronomy 18:18).

That prophet that God will raise up among the Israelite is Jesus. "For unto us a child (Jesus) is born, unto us a Son (Christ) is given, and the government shall be upon his shoulder, and his name shall be call wonderful, counselor, the mighty God, the everlasting Father, the prince of Peace" (Isaiah 9:6). Christ is not Jesus's last name, Jesus means Jehovah is salvation or Jehovah saves. Christ means the anointed one, the Messiah, and the Son of God. When you say Jesus is Lord, you are saying that Jesus is God in the flesh. It took a man to redeem us because sin enter the world by a man. "And the angel said unto her, 'Fear not, Mary, for thou hast found favor with God. And behold thou shalt conceive in thy womb and bring forth a son and shalt call his name Jesus. He shall be great and shall be called the son of the highest, and the Lord God shall give unto him the throne of his Father David. And he shall reign over the house of Jacob (Israel) forever, and his kingdom there shall be no end.' Then said Mary unto the angel, 'How shall this be seeing I know not a man?' And the angel answered and said unto her, 'The Holy Ghost shall come upon thee, and the power of the highest shall overshadow thee, therefore also that holy thing which shall be born of thee shall be called the Son of God" (Luke 1:30–35).

The kingdom is the spiritual church, and the spiritual church is the kingdom. Jesus is King over the kingdom and Lord over the Spiritual church. You have a chose the kingdom of God or the kingdom for God. If you are born again, then you are in God's kingdom; if you are a sinner or religious, then you are in Satan's kingdom. There are two kingdoms, the choice is yours. The different between the birth of Jesus and the birth of a man is that Jesus is the Word of God made flesh. Mary was impregnated by the Word of God. Jesus is pure, holy, and born without sin and without a sin nature just like how Adam was created without a sin nature until he sinned in the garden. Then every man and every woman inherit that sin nature. So every man was born with a sin nature, and that is why we sin by nature. God came in sinful flesh to redeem us from that sinful nature. When a sinner commits a sin, he sins by nature; when a Christian sins, he sins through temptation and yielding to the flesh. "In the beginning was the word (Christ) and the word (Christ) was with God and the word (Christ) was God. The same was in the beginning with God. All things were made by him and without him was not anything made that was made" (John 1:1–3).

The Word of God is God, and the Word of God is Christ. The heavens and earth was created and made by the Word of God, the Word is Spirit and life. The Word of God saves and will cleanse you of your sins and will convict you of your sins. "But as many as received him, to them gave he power to become the sons (children) of God, even to them that believe on his name, which were born, not of blood, nor of the will of the flesh, nor of the will of man, but of God. And the word was made flesh and dwelt among us (and we beheld his glory, the glory as of the only begotten of the Father), full of grace and truth" (John 1:12–14).

The Word of God is spirit and life, only the Word of God can bring conviction. When a religious leader speaks, he will bring no conviction with his words. But when a man speaks the Word of God, he will bring conviction of sin. Because the Word of God is God, and the word was made flesh. "And Joseph also went up from Galilee, out of the city of Nazareth, into Judea unto the city of David, which is called Bethlehem (because he was of the house and lineage of David), to be taxed with Mary, his espoused wife, being great with child. And so it was, that, while they were there, the days were accomplished that she should be delivered. And she brought forth her firstborn son and wrapped him in swaddling clothes and laid him in a manger because there was no room for them in the inn. And there were in the same country shepherds abiding in the field, keeping watch over their flock by night. And, lo, the angel of the Lord came upon them, and the glory of the Lord shone round about them, and they were sore afraid. And the angel said unto them, 'Fear not for behold I bring you good tidings of great joy, which shall be to all people. For unto you is born this day in the city of David a Savior, which is Christ the Lord. And this shall be a sign unto you. Ye shall find the babe wrapped in swaddling clothes, lying in a manger'" (Luke 2:4–12).

The shepherds saw Christ Jesus lying in a manger, and the wise men saw Jesus Christ when he was two in the house. The shepherds and the wise man were not there at the same time. The shepherds were there the day he was born, and the wise men came two years later when Jesus was in a house. The scripture said that Mary brought forth her firstborn son, Jesus, because she had more sons and daughters, but Jesus Christ is God's only begotten Son. Mary and Joseph had more children together, but God is Christ Father because the Word of God was made flesh, Jesus. Jesus Christ was 100 percent man and 100 percent God. When Mary gave birth to Jesus Christ, she was still a virgin, then Joseph and Mary had more children. Because the Word of God said this, "And knew her not till she had brought forth her firstborn son and he called his name Jesus" (Matthew 1:25).

When the Word of God said "and knew her not" means that Joseph had not touch Mary until she gave birth to Jesus. She was a virgin when Jesus was born. Bible critics try to make Jesus just a man, but he was God in human flesh. Jesus had stepbrothers and stepsisters, but Jesus was born of a virgin, Mary's firstborn son. When Mary was conceived by the Word of God, she was a virgin, and she gave birth to Jesus, she was a virgin. Now the birth of Jesus Christ was on this wise when as his mother Mary was espoused to Joseph before they came together, she was found with child of the Holy Ghost. Then Joseph her husband, being a just man and not willing to make her a public example, was minded to put her away privily. But while he thought of these things, behold, the angel of the Lord appeared unto him in a dream, saying, "Joseph, thou son of David, fear not to take unto thee Mary thy wife for that which is conceived in her is of the Holy Ghost. And she shall bring forth a son, and thou shalt call his name Jesus for he shall save his people from their sins. Now all this was done that it might be fulfilled which was spoken of the Lord by the prophet saying, 'Behold, a virgin shall be with child and shall bring forth a son, and they shall call his name Emmanuel, which being interpreted is, God with us'" (Matthew 1:18–23).

The name Jesus means Jehovah is salvation. And Emmanuel means God is with us. And concerning his stepbrothers and stepsisters, the Word of God said this, "Is not this the carpenter's son? Is not his mother called Mary? And his brethren, James and Joses and Simon and Judas? And his sisters, are they not all with us? Whence then hath this man all these things?" (Matthew 13:55–56). The Word of God is of no secret interpretation. God is not trying to trick you, he is trying to save you. The devil and the Bible critics are trying to trick you because the devil is trying to steal your soul. The devil is trying to steal your soul through religion, through trying to work for salvation, through trying to twist up God's word, and confuse you. Now concerning the wise men and the birth of Jesus. The wise men came about two years later, the babe Jesus is now a young child. The Word of God said this, "And when they were come into the house, they saw the young child with Mary his mother and fell down and worshipped him, and when they opened their treasures, they presented unto him gifts: gold and frankincense and myrrh" (Matthew 2:11).

The gold represents Jesus's kingship, the frankincense represents his lordship worship, and the myrrh represents his sacrificial death on the cross for our sins. Remember, the wise men worship this child, and only worship belong to God and not a child. These wise men must have known that this child was God in the flesh, the savior of the whole world. Remember, you cannot join Christianity, you must be birth into Christianity. You can join the church but not Christianity. Because the real church is blood bought by the blood of Jesus Christ. The Word of God said this, "Take heed therefore unto yourselves, and to all the flock, over the which the Holy Ghost hath made you overseers to feed the church of God, which he hath purchased with his own blood" (Acts 20:28). The devil knows that Christianity is the true religion and the body of Christ is the true church. He knows that Jesus is God in the flesh, he knows that Jesus is Lord, and he knows that Jesus is the savior of the world. The Word of God said this, "And in the synagogue, there was a man, which had a spirit of an unclean devil, and cried out with a loud voice, saying, 'Let us alone. What have we to do with thee, thou Jesus of Nazareth art thou come to destroy us? I know thee who thou art, the Holy One of God'" (Luke 4:33–34).

"And always, night and day, he was in the mountains and in the tombs, crying and cutting himself with stones. But when he saw Jesus afar off, he ran and worshipped him and cried with a loud voice and said, 'What have I to do with thee, Jesus, thou Son of the most high God? I adjure thee by God that thou torment me not'" (Mark 5:5–8). Many people believe that there is a God but are not save. You must believe that Jesus is Lord and savior of the world. Just believing in God will not get you into heaven. "Thou believest that there is one God, thou doest well the devils also believe and tremble" (James 2:19). The Israelite believed that there is only one true God and are right, but they did not believe that Jesus was God in the flesh and that Jesus is Lord. The devils believe that there is a God and tremble. When the scripture said that faith without work is dead, it means that works without faith in Jesus is dead because it cannot redeem you, justify you, or declare you righteous, only the faith in Jesus, the finish work of God.

Abraham was justified by his work, and declare righteous, because he believed God and his works by faith justified him because he had offered Isaac upon the altar to God by faith. And God declared him righteous. To be righteous under the law, you had to have kept the whole law and could not keep the whole law because of the sinful nature we have. But Jesus have kept the whole law, and our righteousness is fulfilled in him. "Labor not for the meat which perisheth but for that meat which endureth unto everlasting life, which the son of man shall give unto you for him hath God the Father sealed. Then said they unto him, 'What shall we do that we might work the works of God?' Jesus answered and said unto them, 'This is the work of God, that ye believe on him whom he hath sent'" (John 6:27–29).

No one could keep the whole law to declare himself righteous, not Abraham, Isaac, Jacob, Moses, David, or the prophets. So, God came in the flesh and kept the whole law and nail the law to his cross. "And you, being dead in your sins and the uncircumcision of your flesh, hath he quickened (made alive) together with him, having forgiven you all trespasses, blotting out the handwriting of ordinance that was against us, which was contrary to us, and took it out of the way, nailing it to his cross" (Colossians 2:13–14). "For whosoever shall the whole law and yet offend in one point, he is guilty of all" (James 2:10). That is why Jesus told those the Pharisees which caught the woman in adultery, "He that is without sin, let him cast the first stone." They might have not committed adultery, but they may have been liars, haters, backbiters, murderers, drunker, fornicators, and thieves. So, they were just as guilty as the woman caught in adultery. Because everyone that get save by grace, not the law, is a sinner. Everyone is guilty before God because everyone has sin, and we need a savior. "In hope of eternal life, which God, that cannot lie, promised before the world began but hath in due times manifested his word through preaching, which is committed unto me according to the commandment of God, our savior. To Titus, mine own son after the common faith, grace, mercy, and peace from God the Father and the Lord Jesus Christ our Savior" (Titus 1:2–4).

Notice the Word of God, said that God is our savior and that the Lord Jesus Christ is our savior. You have God the Father, God the Son, and God the Holy Ghost. Christ is God, and Jesus is Lord. "These words spake Jesus and lifted up his eyes to heaven, and said, 'Father, the hour (time) is come. Glorify thy son, that thy Son also may glorify thee as thou hast given him power over all flesh that he should give eternal life to as many as thou hast given him. And this is life eternal, that they might know thee the only true God, and Jesus Christ, whom thou hast sent. I have glorified thee on earth. I have finished the work which thou gavest me to do. And now, O Father, glorify thou me with thine own self with the glory which I had with thee before the world was'" (John 17:1–5). This is called the Lord's pray. Jesus know that his time is at hand to go to the cross, to redeem the whole world that believeth. Not just for the United State of America, but for the whole world. He died for North America,

South America, Africa, Europe, Asia, Australia, Israel, Saudi Arabia. Jesus is the savior of the world.

Remember, God only have one church, which is the spiritual church, the body of Jesus Christ. This church is a body of believer in Jesus Christ. There is one God, one Father, one Lord, one faith, one baptism, and one church. Jesus will be your savior or your judge. Remember, religion cannot save you or forgive you, work cannot save you, neither can you work off sin. Nothing but the blood of Jesus. You must be blood bought and blood wash. And the blood of Jesus has signed your name in the lamb book of life. "And the seventy returned again with joy, saying, 'Lord, even the devils are subject unto us through thy name.' And he said unto them, 'I beheld Satan as lightning fall from heaven. Behold, I give unto you power to tread on serpents and scorpions and over all the power of the enemy, and nothing shall by any means hurt you. Notwithstanding in this rejoice not that the spirits are subject unto you but rather rejoice because your names are written in heaven (lamb's book of life)'" (Luke 10:17–20).

Jesus Christ saw Satan fell from heaven as lightning, that is how fast God kicked Satan out of heaven after rebelling against him in heaven. So, if Jesus Christ saw Satan fall from heaven, that mean he was there before the foundation of the world. "But if I tarry long, that thou mayest know how thou oughtest to be have thyself in the house of God, which is the church of the living God, the pillar and ground of the truth. And without controversy great is the mystery of godliness. God was manifest in the flesh, justified in the Spirit, seen of angels, preached unto the Gentiles, believed on in the world, received up into glory" (1 Timothy 3:15–16). You cannot go to heaven in sin, someone have to atone for your sin, and someone have to bear your sins. Jesus is our sin bearer, and that sin bearer must be holy and without sin. That someone must be born without a sin nature, that someone could never have sin. He cannot redeem you if he needs to be redeemed. Jesus never asks for forgiveness to God because he is God in the flesh. God is the Word of God made flesh, Jesus is the word made flesh. God the Father, God the Son, God the Holy Ghost, you cannot separate the three because they are one and the same. You cannot have God without having Jesus, and to have God in your life, you must believe that Jesus is Lord and that he died in the cross for your sins, anything beside that is a lie.

"I have not written unto because ye know not the truth but because ye know it, and that no lie is of the truth. Who is a liar but he that denieth that Jesus is the Christ (Lord)? He is Antichrist that denieth the Father and the Son. Whosoever denieth the Son (Jesus), the same hath not the Father, [but] he that acknowledgeth the Son (Jesus) hath the Father also" (1 John 2:21–23). Jesus is Lord, and someday, the Word of God said. "That at the name of Jesus, every knee should bow of things in heaven and things in earth and things under the earth. And that every tongue should confess that Jesus is Lord to the glory of God the Father" (Philippians 2:10–11).

Every sinner's knee shall bow, every religious leader's knee shall bow, every demon shall bow, every dictator shall bow, Satan shall bow, and every Christian shall bow. Every mouth shall confess that Jesus is Lord to the glory of God the Father. God is a loving God, God is a good God, and God is a merciful God, and God wishes that none should perish but that all should come to repentance. Black, white, rich, or poor, male or female, he wishes that all come to repentance. Then Peter opened his mouth, and said, "Of a truth I perceive that God is no respecter of persons. But in every nation he that feareth him and worketh righteousness is accepted with him. The word which God sent unto the children of Israel, preaching peace by Jesus Christ (he is Lord of all)" (Acts 10:34–36). There is authority in the name of Jesus. Authority is another name for power. Authority means the power or right to enforce obedience. Demons come to obedience in the name of Jesus. Demons tremble at the name of Jesus. Satan trembles at the name of Jesus. There is save power in the name of Jesus, there is healing power in the name of Jesus. "Neither is there salvation in any other for there is none other name under heaven given among men, whereby we must be saved" (Acts 4:12).

There is only one name that can save, and that is the name of Jesus. There is no authority in religious leader's name. There is no saving power in religion, except for one, the religion of Christianity. After the resurrection of the Lord Jesus Christ, the disciples had told

Thomas that they had seen the Lord, but Thomas did not believe them. So, the Lord had appeared to Thomas and the disciples eight days later that evening. "Then saith he to Thomas, 'Reach hither thy finger and behold my hands and reach hither thy hand and trust it into my side, and be not faithless but believing.' And Thomas answered and said unto him, 'My Lord and my God.' Jesus saith unto him, 'Thomas, because Thou hast seen me, thou hast believed, blessed are they that have not seen and yet have believed.' And many other signs truly did Jesus in the presence of his disciples, which are not written in this book. But these are written, that ye might believe that Jesus is the Christ, the Son of God, and that believing ye might have life through his name" (John 20:27–31).

To receive salvation, you must receive it by faith; to serve the Lord, you must serve him by faith because the just must live by faith. The Pharisees and religious leader of that day did not believed that Jesus was Son of God and savior of the world, but he is. He is the savior of the whole world, not part of it, but the whole world. "And he said unto them, 'Ye are from beneath, I am from above. Ye are of this world, I am not of this world. I said therefore unto you that ye shall die in your sins for if ye believe not that I am he, ye shall die in your sins'" (John 8:23–24). When Jesus died of the cross, he said it is finish. That means that the plan of salvation through him is finish. You cannot be redeemed, no other was, except through the blood of Jesus, which he shed on the cross for the whole world. Jesus said, "I am alpha and omega, the beginning and the ending, the first and the last." That means no one can come after him and say I am the savior of the world without lying after the resurrection of the Lord Jesus Christ. He commissioned his disciples to preached the gospel to all nations, beginning at Jerusalem. "And he said unto them, 'These are the words which I spake unto you, while I was yet with you, that all things must be fulfilled which were written in the law of Moses and in the prophets and in the psalms, concerning me.' Then opened he their understanding, that they might understand the scriptures, and said unto them, 'Thus it is written, and thus it behooved Christ to suffer and to rise from the dead the third day and that repentance and remission (forgiveness) of sins should be preached in his name among all nations beginning at Jerusalem. And ye are witnesses of these things'" (Luke 24:44–48).

"And when they saw him, they worshipped him, but some doubted. And Jesus came and spake unto them saying, 'All power (authority) is given unto me in heaven and in earth. Go ye therefore and teach all nations, baptizing them in the name of the Father and of the Son and of the Holy Ghost, teaching them to observe all things whatsoever I have commanded you. And, lo, I am with you always, even unto the end of the world. Amen'" (Matthew 28:17–20). "And he said unto them, 'Go ye into all the world and preach the gospel to every creature. He that believeth and is baptized shall be saved, but he that believeth not shall be damned'" (Mark 16:15–16).

The apostles bear witness that Jesus is the savior of the world, and the apostles bear witness of his death, burial, and resurrection from the dead. The law of Moses bear witness that he is the savior, the psalms, and the prophets bear witness that he is the savior. The gospel of Matthew, Mark, and Luke have the great commission. Jesus commissioned to preach the gospel because the gospel saves. "And as he sat upon the Mount of Olives, the disciples came unto him privately, saying, 'Tell us, when shall these things be? And what shall be the sign of thy coming and of the end of the world?' And Jesus answered and said unto them, 'Take heed that no man deceive you. For many shall come in my name, saying, I am Christ and shall deceive many'" (Matthew 24:3–5). "And many false prophets shall rise and shall deceive many." (Matthew 24:11).

What is a false Christ? A false Christ is a false Messiah, a false deliverer. Christ is the true deliverer of God because he came into the world to save that which was lost. A false prophet is a false messenger of Satan. He preaches a false gospel, preaches another way to go to heaven except through Jesus. A prophet of God preach the gospel of Jesus Christ, the only way to go to heaven and to be saved. Satan's job is to deceive you through false religion and false doctrines. "This is a faithful saying and worthy of all acceptation that Christ Jesus came into the world to save sinners of whom I am chief. Howbeit for this cause I obtained mercy that in me first Jesus Christ might show forth all long-suffering, for a pattern to them which should hereafter believe on him to life everlasting" (1 Timothy 1:15–16). "For this is good and acceptable in the sight of God our Savior who will have all men to be saved and to come unto the knowledge of the truth. For there is one God and one mediator between God and men, the man Christ Jesus who gave himself a ransom for all to be testified in due time" (1 Timothy 2:3–6).

Only a true and living God can save the whole world from eternal damnation that believed in the name of Jesus. God is the only one that can save mankind from there sin. Because God is holy and without sin. Remember, neither religion nor works nor water can wash away sin, nothing but the blood of Jesus. God have made provision for our salvation through Jesus Christ. "Herein is love, not that we loved God but that he loved us and sent his Son to be the propitiation for our sins" (1 John 4:10). Propitiation means the perfect sacrifice for sin, which appeased God and satisfied God's justice, reconciling God and man, offering believing sinners perfect righteousness. The Word of God says this, "Hereby know we that we dwell in him and he is us because he hath given us of his Spirit. And we have seen and do testify that the Father sent the Son to be the savior of the world. Whosoever shall confess that Jesus is the Son of God, God dwelleth in him and he in God" (1 John 4:13–15). Whose record are you going to believe, the record of man which say you can go to heaven another way, or the record of God which say Jesus Christ is the only way to God? When comparing the record of God with the record of man, there is no comparison because the record of God cannot lie, but man can. The Apostle Paul asked this question at the Church of Romans, "For what if some did not believe? Shall their unbelief make the faith of God without effect? God forbids. Yea, let God be true but every man a liar" (Romans 3:3–4).

"Paul, a servant of God, and an apostle of Jesus Christ, according to the faith of God's elect and the acknowledging of the truth which is after godliness. In hope of eternal life, which God, that cannot lie, promised before the world began but hath in due times manifested his word through preaching, which is committed unto me according to the commandment of God our Savior" (Titus 1:1–4). You see, God is our savior in human flesh, which die on the cross to redeem us. Do not let the devil lie to you by telling you another way through religion. By God's grace and his mercy, he saved us, not by any goodness of our own. But by his grace, his unmerited favor, and compassion which he gave us. If we receive the witness a deceiver and an Antichrist, look to yourselves that we lose not those things which we have wrought but that we receive a full reward. "Whosoever transgresseth, and abideth not in the doctrine of Christ, hath not God. He that abideth in the doctrine of Christ, he hath both the Father and the Son. If there come any unto you, and bring not this doctrine, receive him not into your house, neither bid him God speed for he that biddeth him God speed is partaker of his evil deeds" (2 John 1:9–11).

This is the only doctrine of the church (body of Christ), the true church and the true doctrine which is the death, burial, and resurrection of Jesus Christ; with this doctrine, you have a false church. You must believe that God rapped himself up in a human flesh to redeem us. Church doctrine is sometimes man-made doctrine. You have the doctrine and add a Jesus. Add a Jesus to believe that Jesus is Lord and add something else to it, and the doctrine of exit Jesus is this: good works but no death of Jesus on the cross, no burial of Jesus in the grave, and no resurrection of Jesus Christ from the grave. The doctrine of Jesus saves the doctrine of the devil deceives. "Now the Spirit speaketh expressly that in the latter times, some shall depart from the faith (Christianity), giving heed to seducing spirits and doctrines of devils, speaking lies in hypocrisy, having their conscience seared with a hot iron, forbidding to marry, and commanding to abstain from meats, which God hath created to be received with thanksgiving of them which believe and know the truth. For every creature of God is good, and nothing to be refused if it be received with thanksgiving for it is sanctified by the Word of God and prayer" (1 Timothy 4:1–5).

What are doctrines of devil? A doctrine of devil is a doctrine that says you can go to heaven or be saved some other way than through Jesus Christ. There are many false doctrines right now. Doctrine means teachings of the truth of Jesus, or false teaching of the devil. Doctrine of devils seems right if you do not know the truth, and the reason you do not know the truth is because you are spiritually blind. Once you are born again, your eyes are open and you will know the truth through studying God's word. Doctrines of devil are design to deceive you, and the way it deceives is by the lack of knowledge. "Study to show thyself approved unto God, a workman that needeth not to be ashamed righty dividing the word of truth" (2 Timothy 3:15)." Marriage is honorable in all and the bed undefiled, but whoremongers and adulterers God will judge" (Hebrews 13:4). When you forbid to marriage and live together, you are living in fornication which is a sin, that means you are living in sin. Only marriage between a man and a woman is honorable before God. That is the only marriage God honors.

And to abstain from meats, you can be a vegetarian and still be a Christian. There is no salvation in meat or vegetable. Do not lose your soul over meat or vegetable. "For the kingdom of God is not meat and drink but righteousness and peace and joy in the Holy Ghost" (Roman 14:17). We must get knowledge of the Lord Jesus Christ because knowledge is power, and to have a good foundation in Jesus, you must have knowledge. Some believer does not have a good foundation or no foundation at all, some will depart from the faith, Christianity. "They went out from us, but they were not of us for if they had been of us, they would no doubt have continued with us, but they went out that they might be made manifest that they were not all of us" (1 John 2:19).

"Therefore whosoever heareth these sayings of mine, and doeth them, I will liken him unto a wise man, which built his house upon a rock. And the rain descended and the flood came and the winds blew and beat upon that house, and it fell not for it was founded upon a rock. And every one that heareth these sayings of mine, and doeth them not, shall be likened unto a foolish man which built his house upon the sand. And the rain descended and the floods came and the winds blew and beat upon the house, and it fell and great was the fall of it. And it came to pass, when Jesus had ended these sayings, the people were astonished at his doctrine" (Matthew 7:24–28).

For us to be able to stand in the Christian faith, and not fall away, we must have a good foundation in the faith. To have a good foundation in the faith, you must study your Bible. Go to Bible study and have good teaching because you have all wind of doctrine and feel-good gospel. Salvation is an invitation to accept Jesus as savior and Lord. You have a choice, accept the invitation or reject the invitation to go to heaven, marvel not you must be born again. Jesus gave a parable about the wedding feast, which also is called the marriage supper of the lamb. When you are born again, you are married to Jesus, and Jesus is married to you. Jesus have this invitation to the wedding feast. "And Jesus answered and spake unto them again by parables and said, 'The kingdom of heaven is like unto a certain king (God), which made a marriage for his son (Jesus), and sent forth his servants (preaches) to call them that were bidden to the wedding, and they would not come. Again, he sent forth other servants, saying, "Tell them which are bidden. Behold, I have prepared my dinner, my oxen and my fatlings are killed, and all things are ready. Come unto the marriage." But they made light of it and went their ways, once to his farm, another to his merchandise. And the remnant took his servants and entreated them spitefully and slew them. But when the king heard thereof, he was wroth, and he sent forth his armies and destroyed those murderers and burned up their city. Then saith he to his servants, "The wedding is ready, but they which were bidden were not worthy"'" (Matthew 22:1–8).

The Jews are God-chosen people, but God said that they were not worthy to come to the marriage supper of the lamb because they killed the prophets and rejected Jesus Christ as Savior and Lord. "He came unto his own, and his own received him not. But as many as received him to them gave he power (authority) to become the sons (children) of God, even to them that believe on his name" (John 1:11–12). Since the Jews rejected the invitation of God to the marriage supper of the lamb, so God said, "Go out into the world and preach the gospel to everyone. To the drunkard, to the liars, to the adulterer, to the fornicators, to the murderer, and to all that are unclean by sin. And to come to the marriage supper of the lamb, way the table is spread, and the feast of the Lord is going on, and where you will never die, but receive eternal life."

"Go ye therefore into the highways and as many as ye shall find bid to the marriage. So those servants went out into the highways and gathered together all as many as they found, both bad and good, and the wedding was furnished with guests. And when the king came in to see the guests, he saw there a man which had not on a wedding garment, and he saith unto him, 'Friend, how camest thou in hither not having a wedding garment?' And he was speechless. Then said the king to the servants, 'Bind him hand and foot and take him away and cast him into outer darkness, there shall be weeping and gnashing of teeth. For many are called but few are chosen'" (Matthew 22:9–14).

The marriage supper of the lamb will be in heaven. The man wants to be at the marriage supper of the lamb, but he had on the wrong garment because he rejected the invitation of God unto salvation which is the gospel of Jesus Christ. He should have had on the garment of righteousness, but instead, he had on the garment of self-righteousness, which is religion and works of righteousness. The man wanted to go to heaven without being saved; but to go to heaven, you must be born again because everyone in this kingdom or church will be dressed alike. We will be clothed in righteousness, not self-righteousness. And having our wedding garments spotless and washed in the blood of the lamb. The garment that the man had on was spotted with sin, that is why he was not accepted at the wedding feast. He rejected the invitation of salvation, and God rejected him at the marriage supper of the lamb. You must first be married to the lamb of God before you can come to the marriage supper. The church is the bride and Jesus is the bridegroom, we are married to Jesus through the gospel. Without the wedding garment, you cannot go to heaven.

God told the angel to cast him into the lake of fire, where there shall be weeping and gnashing of teeth, because he was not married to Jesus. "For the husband is the head of the wife, even as Christ is the head of the church, and he is the savior of the body. Therefore, as the church is subject unto Christ, so let the wives be to their own husband in everything. Husbands, love your wives even as Christ also loved the church and gave himself for it. That he might sanctify and cleanse it with the washing of water by the word, that he might present it to himself a glorious church, not having spot or wrinkle or any such thing, but that it should be holy and without blemish" (Ephesians 5:23–27)

Christianity is more than a religion, it is a relationship with God through Jesus Christ. Jesus died for the church, the church is blood bought and blood washed, and we are sanctified through the truth, which is the Word of God. And we are sealed and kept through the Holy Spirit until the day of redemption. Christ Jesus is coming back for a saved and sanctified church, not a religious church or a sinful one. "Let us be glad and rejoice and give honor to him for the marriage of the lamb is come, and his wife hath made herself ready. And to her was granted that she should be arrayed in fine linen, clean and white, for the fine linen is the righteousness of saints. And he saith unto me, 'Write, blessed are they which are called unto the marriage supper of the lamb.' And he saith unto me, 'These are the true sayings of God'" (Revelation 19:7–9). None but the righteous shall see God. Marvel not you must be born again, the devil have a false religion, the devil have a false gospel, the devil have a false doctrine, and the devil have a false message that pastors across America offer this invitation to salvation every Sunday morning, so there is no excuse to be save.

God is a just God. He is a righteous God, he is a holy God, he is merciful God, he is a good God. Do not let the hearse bring you to church or wait until it is too late because God will judge the world in righteousness someday. There is none good but God, there is none worthy to be save, only by his grace and mercy he provides us this salvation. God hears two kind of prayers, the sinner's prayer unto salvation, repent of your sins and accept Jesus Christ as Savior and Lord. And God hears the prayer of the righteous because Jesus Christ is our righteousness; therefore, God hears our prayers. Why do we pray? We pray for forgiveness, we pray for strength, we pray for others, we pray for provision, and we pray for divine protection. We pray to the Father to forgive our sins because the Father said, "If we confess our sins, he is faithful and just to forgive us our sins and to cleanse us from all righteousness. If we say that we have not sinned, we make him a liar, and his word is not in us" (1 John 1:9–10).

When you become a Christian, that does not mean that you will not sin. But when you sin against God, you will be out of fellowship with God. To get back in fellowship with God, you must confess your sins to God, not a man, only God can forgive sin, and only the blood of Jesus can cleanse it. "This then is the message which we have heard of him, and declare unto you, that God is light (holy) and in him is no darkness (sin) at all. If we say that we have fellowship with him and walk (live) in darkness (sin), we lie and do not the truth, but if we walk in the light, as he is in the light, we have fellowship one with another, and the blood of Jesus Christ his Son cleanseth us from all sin. If we say that we have no sin, we deceive ourselves, and the truth is not in us" (1 John 1:5–8).

If you are sinner, then you are out of fellowship with God. If you are part of a religion, you are out of fellowship with God because you are still in your sin. Because something must die and atone for your sin. Jesus is the only perfect sacrifice of God. That is why he is the savior of the world because he is the perfect sacrifice of God. God do not hear sinner's prayers or religious prayers, only Christian prayers because there is only one God, one heavenly Father, one Lord, one faith, and one baptism. God wants us to live holy because he is holy. God wants us to walk in the light, not in darkness because God is light, not darkness. Satan is darkness, and he is the prince of darkness. So, who is your father, God or Satan? "My little children, these things write I unto you, that ye sin not. And if any man sin, we have an advocate with the Father, Jesus Christ the righteous. And he is the propitiation (atonement) for our sins and not for ours only but also for the sins of the whole world" (1 John 2:1–2).

Jesus Christ is our advocate, that means he represent us and speaks for us on his behave to God when we pray to the Father for forgiveness of sins and for his blessing. That is why he said, "I am the way, the truth, and the life. No man cometh unto the Father but by me." When we pray, we must pray in the name of Jesus; when we receive salvation, we receive it in the name of Jesus; and when we go to heaven, it is in the name of Jesus. Jesus is our propitiation, that means he is our atonement for our sins, the perfect sacrifice of God, holy, pure, righteous, undefiled, and never have sinned. God can and will forgive you of every sin that you have committed in Jesus's name except for one sin, and that is blasphemy of the Holy Ghost. "Wherefore I say unto you, all manner of sin and blasphemy shall be forgiven unto me, but the blasphemy against the Holly Ghost shall not be forgiven unto men" (Matthew 12:31).

So do not let the devil tell you, that you have sin too much, and that the sins you have committed cannot not be forgiven. Everyone that got saved was a sinner to the outmost Jesus saved. This is why he came into the world, to save sinners. There is no big sin and little sin, all unrighteousness is sin. "What shall we say then? Shall we continue in sin that grace may abound? God forbids. How shall we that are dead to sin live any longer there in?" (Romans 6:1–2). When we are a Christian, we do not practice sin just because we can get forgiveness for our sins by the grace of God. Christians may sin from time to time, but Christians do not live in sin. Because we have been freed from the bondage of sin. When a Christian sins, they sin through temptation, but when a sinner sins, he sins because he is bound by sin, he is still in bondage to sin. Sinners sin by nature because he has a sin nature, which he received through the fall of Adam. Christians have been freed from the bondage of sin and our sin nature by the blood of Jesus. "Know ye not that so many of us as were baptized into Jesus Christ were baptized into his death? Therefore, we are buried with him by baptism into death. That like as Christ was raised up from the dead by the glory of the Father even so we also should walk in newness of life. For if we have been planted together in the likeness of his death, we shall be also in the likeness of his resurrection. Knowing this that our old man is crucified with him that the body of sin might be destroyed, that henceforth we should not serve sin" (Romans 6:3–6).

Water baptism cannot save you or wash away your sins, it is symbolic of the death, burial, and resurrection of Jesus Christ. And it symbolizes that the old man is dead and buried with Jesus Christ through water baptism and that you have turn your back on the world. By being raised from water baptism means you are going to walk in newness of your life as a Christian, that is Christian baptism. Being baptized after you have received Jesus Christ as Savior and Lord, John baptism is baptism unto repentance. "Let not sin therefore reign in your mortal body that ye should obey it in the lust thereof. Neither yield ye your members as instruments of unrighteousness unto sin but yield yourselves unto God as those that are alive from the dead and your members as instruments of righteousness unto God. For sin shall not have dominion over you for ye are not under the law but under grace" (Romans 6:12–14).

Under the law, we were in bondage to sin because the law could not free us from the bondage of sin. But under grace, we have been freed from the bondage of sin by the blood of Jesus Christ to those that believe. Now as a Christian, we should not let sin reign in our body and in our lives. When we sin, we should confess our sin to God right away and be cleanse by the blood of Jesus. If sin reigns in our body, we will obey that sin more than obeying God. We cannot be a servant God and a servant of sin. We should not let sin dominate our lives as Christians. "Being then made free from sin, ye became the servants of righteousness" (Romans 6:18). When we sin as a Christian, we sin by temptation, by weakness of the flesh, and by our human nature (infirmity). God's mercy is renewed every morning, so never think that God is angry with you when you sin, God may not be pleased, but he still loves you. Never run from God when you sin, but rather run to God to be forgiven of your sins. "For the wages of sin is death, but the gift of God is eternal life through Jesus Christ our Lord" (Romans 6:23).

You have a choice: eternal death, which is the lake of fire, or eternal life, which is through our Lord and Savior Jesus Christ. God is a good God and a merciful God. God is not like people when he forgives your sins, God remembers them no more. God wants us to live holy and pure as a Christian. "He hath not dealt with us after our sins nor rewarded us according to our iniquities. For as the heaven is high above the earth, so great is his mercy toward them that fear him. As far as the east is from the west, so far hath he removed our transgressions from us" (Psalm 103:10–12). "He will turn again, he will have compassion upon us, he will subdue our iniquities, and thou wilt cast all their sins into the depths of the sea" (Micah 7:19). "'Come now, and let us reason together,' saith the Lord. Though your sins be as scarlet, they shall be as white as snow; though they be red like crimson, they shall be as wool" (Isaiah 1:18). "I, even I, am he that blotteth out thy transgressions for mine own sake and will not remember thy sins" (Isaiah 43:25).

When God forgives your sins, God forgives all your sins, not some of your sins, and God will not remember your sins to hold it against you later. For God to hear and forgive your sin, you must be a worshipper of God, that means you must be saved because God do not hear sinner's prayer. "Now we know that God heareth not sinners, but if any man be a worshipper of God, and doeth his will, him he heareth" (John 9:31).

What does worship means? Worship means expression of the relationship between believers and God, it involves reverence and adoration of God. To worship the true and living God, you must be born again. You cannot worship the true and living God as a sinner because no sin shall dwell in the present. You can praise God as a sinner because the Word of God said, "Let everything that have breath praise the Lord because he is worthy to be praised." Once again, Christianity is more than a religion, it is a relationship with God through the blood of Jesus Christ our Lord and Savior. We are in covenant with God through the blood of Jesus Christ, which is a blood covenant. So, our relationship with God is bonded in the blood of Jesus. Jesus is more than our Savior and Lord, he is our high priest, and Jesus is our intercessor. Jesus is our advocate, and Jesus is our mediator. What does high priest mean? It means the head priest or the high priest over the house of God. "And having a high priest over the house of God (church), let us draw near with a true heart in full assurance of faith, having our hearts sprinkled from an evil conscience and our body washed with pure water (word) of God" (Hebrews 10:21–22).

Jesus is the only high priest over the church, the body of believer in Jesus Christ. There is only one savior of the world which can cleanse your sins by his blood. There is only one high priest that can atone for your sins, and there is only one church that will go to heaven, the Christian Church, because that church is blood bought and blood washed. What does intercessor mean? Intercessor means prayer offered in behalf of other. When we pray to God in the name of Jesus for forgiveness of our sins, Jesus intercede on our behalf to the Father, and our sins are forgiven. "That whatsoever ye shall ask of the Father in my name, he may give it you" (John 15:16). "For we are saved by hope (faith). But hope that is seen is not hope (faith) for what a man seeth, why doeth he yet hope for? But if we hope for that we see not, then do we with patience wait for it. Likewise, the Spirit also helpeth our infirmities for we know not what we should pray for as we ought, but the Spirit itself maketh intercession for us with groanings which cannot be uttered, and he that searcheth the hearts knoweth what is the mind of the Spirit because he maketh intercession for the saints according to the will of God" (Romans 8:24–27).

Jesus intercedes to God through the Holy Spirit which dwells in all born-again believer. To be God's children, you must have his Holy Spirit. "Now if any man have not the Spirit of Christ, he is none of his" (Romans 8:9). Jesus is our advocate. What does advocate means? Advocate means that Jesus speaks or represents us as believers by the right of election, by redemption, by regeneration, by inputted righteousness, and by justification. "My little children, these things write I unto you, that ye sin not. And if any man sin, we have an advocate with the Father, Jesus Christ the righteous. And he is the propitiation for our sins and not for our only but also for the sins of the whole world" (1 John 2:1–2). "And the Lord said, 'Simon, Simon, behold, Satan hath desired to have you, that he may sift you as wheat. But I have prayed for thee that thy faith fail not, and when thou art converted, strengthen thy brethren" (Luke 22:31–32).

What is a mediator? A mediator is a go-between, the man in the middle. Christ is our mediator as the one who reconciles us to God. Because our sin has separated us from God. Jesus is our go-between. Jesus is our man in the middle. "For this is good and acceptable in the sight of God our Savior who will have all men to be saved and to come unto the knowledge of the truth. For there is one God and one mediator between God and men, the man Christ Jesus, who gave himself a random for all to be testified in due time" (1 Timothy 2:3–6).

You cannot go to God for nothing, except you go through Jesus because he is our mediator, he is our go-between God and man, and he is the man in the middle. No man or woman can be a mediator on this earth but the Lord Jesus Christ. No man or woman is holy enough to be the mediator between God and man. Jesus is the only one because Jesus purchase the church, the body of believer with his own blood. "But now hath he obtained a more excellent ministry by how much also he is the mediator of a better covenant, which was established upon better promises. For if that first covenant had been faultless, then should no place have been sought for the second" (Hebrews 8:6–7). "And for this cause he is the mediator of the new testament that by means of death for the redemption of the transgressions that were under the first testament, they which are called might receive the promise of eternal inheritance (life)" (Hebrews 9:15).

"To the general assembly and church of the firstborn (Jesus), which are written in heaven, and to God the judge of all and to the spirits of just men made perfect and to Jesus the mediator of the new covenant and to the blood of sprinkling that speaketh better things than that of Abel" (Hebrews 12:23–24). Jesus is the door to go to heaven. If any man come another way, he is a thief and a robber. Jesus is too high, you cannot go over him. Jesus is too low, you cannot go under him. Jesus is too wide, you cannot go around him, you must come through the door. "Then said Jesus unto them again, 'Verily, verily, I say unto you, I am the door of the sheep. All that ever came before me are thieves and robbers, but the sheep did not hear them. I am the door. By me if any man enters in, he shall be saved and shall go in and out and find pasture" (John 10:7–9).

Jesus is the door to heaven, and the gospel of Jesus Christ is the key through faith. We are saved through grace by faith, not by works. "Wherefore we receiving a kingdom (church) which cannot be moved, let us have grace, whereby we may serve God acceptably with reverence and godly fear for our God is a consuming fire" (Hebrews 12:28–29).

# We Worship God through Jesus

Why did God create man? God created us to worship him. God had created Lucifer and all the angel in heaven to worship him. But Lucifer was lifted up with pride and rebelled against God and persuaded one third of the angels in heaven to rebelled with him against God. So, God cast Lucifer and the one third of angel out of heaven. "How art thou fallen from heaven, o Lucifer, son of the morning! How art thou cut down to the ground, which didst weaken the nations! For thou hast said in thine heart, 'I will ascend into heaven, I will exalth my throne above the star of God. I will sit also upon the mount of the congregation in the sides of the north. I will ascend above the heights of the clouds. I will be like the most High.' Yet thou shalt be brought down to hell to the sides of the pit" (Isaiah 14:12–15).

"And the seventy return again with joy, saying, 'Lord, even the devils are subject unto us through thy name.' And he said unto them, 'I beheld Satan as lightning fall from heaven. Behold, I give unto you power to tread on serpents and scorpions and over all the power of the enemy, and nothing shall by any means hurt you. Notwithstanding in this rejoice not, that the spirits are subject unto you but rather rejoice because your names are written in heaven'" (Luke 10:17–20). Lucifer had forgotten who was the creature and who were the creator. Lucifer was the most beautiful angel that God had created. He was the cherubim that covered. He was the cherubim that covered the throne of God. He was the highest-ranking angel in heaven. He was the forth in charge in heaven, only God the Father and God the Son and God the Holy Ghost he had to answered to. He was the director of the heavenly choir. And then, he was life up with pride because of his beauty. He became drunk with power. He thought that he could run heaven better then God.

"Thou hast been in Eden, the garden of God. Every precious stone was thy covering, the sardius, topaz, and the diamond, the beryl, the onyx, and the jasper, the sapphire, the emerald, and the carbuncle, and gold. The workmanship of thy tabrets and of thy pipes was prepared in thee in the day that thou wast created. Thou art the anointed cherub that covereth, and I have set thee so thou wast upon the holy mountain of God. Thou hast walked up and down in the midst of the stones of fire. Thou wast perfect in thy ways from the day that thou wast created till iniquity was found in thee. By the multitude of thy merchandise they have filled the midst of thee with violence, and thou hast sinned; therefore, I will cast thee as profane out of the mountain of God, and I will destroy thee, o covering cherub, from the midst of the stone of fire. Thine heart was lifted up because of thy beauty. Thou hast corrupted thy wisdom by reason of thy brightness. I will cast thee to the ground, I will lay thee before kings that they may behold thee" (Ezekiel 28:13–17).

And after the rebellion of Satan and one third of the angel, God decided to create human being to worship him. This is why Satan hates Christian because we took his place in worshipping God. Every time we praise and worship God, we give him a black eye because he remembers when he was the director of the heavenly choir, that is why Satan hates praise and worship, and Satan always causes trouble in the choir. He does that to stop us from praising God because Satan knows that there is only one true God that is worthy of praise and worship. "Lord, thou hast been our dwelling place in all generations. Before the mountains were brought forth or ever thou hadst formed the earth and the world, even from everlasting to everlasting, thou art God" (Psalm 90:1–2).

"The earth is the Lord's, and the fullness thereof, the world and they that dwell therein. For he hath founded it upon the seas and established it upon the floods. Who shall ascend into the hilt of the Lord? Or who shall stand in his holy place? He that hath clean hands and a pure heart who hath not lifted up his soul unto vanity nor sworn deceitfully. He shall receive the blessing from the Lord and righteousness from the God of his salvation" (Psalm 24:1–5). "God created the heaven and the earth" (Genesis 1:1–28). Thus, the heavens and the earth were finished, and all the host of them. And on the seventh day, God ended his work which he had made, and he rested on the seventh day from all his work which he had made. And God blessed the seventh day and sanctified it because that in it he had rested from all his work which God created and made.

Now when God had rested on the seventh, or the Sabbath day, he did not rest because he was tired because God do not and cannot get tired and because God neither sleep or slumber. God is a spirit, not flesh and blood, flesh and blood gets tired, but spirit cannot. God had rested from all his work after he created the heavens and the earth. He then rested from all his labor on the seventh day or Sabbath day, then he sanctified it and hollowed it for a day of rest. This is the creation of Sabbath, and you have the Jewish Sabbath, which is a day of rest and worship. There is only one Sabbath day. Sabbath means seventh, so the Sabbath day is for rest and worship. Jesus Christ is our rest, and we worship God through the relationship we have with Jesus Christ, our Savior and Lord. Jesus have kept the whole law, including the Sabbath day, so when we become a Christian, that means we have kept the whole law through Jesus, and then Jesus become of rest and righteousness. We worship God through Jesus on Sunday because Jesus rose from the dead on Sunday, the Holy Ghost came on Sunday. When God created man, he created us to worship him. After kicking Satan and the fallen angels out of heaven, he could have created more angels to worship him, but instead, he created human being to worship him. Angels are a spirit, human beings are spirit, flesh, and soul.

"And God said, 'Let us make man in our image, after our likeness, and let them have dominion over the fish of the sea and over the fowl of the air and over the cattle and over all the earth and over every creeping thing the creepeth upon the earth.' So, God created man in his own image. In the image of God created he him, male and female created he them. And God blessed them, and God said unto them, 'Be fruitful and multiply and replenish the earth'" (Genesis 1:26–28). The first man that God had created was the spirit man because God said, "Let us (Father, Son, Holy Ghost) make man in our image or likeness." God is a Spirit, not flesh and blood, so for man to be in God image or likeness, he had to be spirit. "And the Lord God formed man of the dust of the ground, and breathed into his nostrils the breath of life, and man became a living soul" (Genesis 2:7).

This is the fleshly man that God formed from the ground and breed the breath of life into his nostrils and the breath of life which is the Holy Ghost to quicken his spirit man, and he became a living soul. Man is flesh, spirit, and soul. God quickens the spirit and saves your soul, and the flesh returns back to the ground. Do not listen to that lie Satan is telling that when you are dead, you are done, and there is no judgment for your sins or we evolved from monkeys and apes. We were created by God to worship God. We took Satan and the fallen angels' place in heaven. "Our father worshipped in this mount, and ye say that in Jerusalem is the place where men ought to worship. Jesus saith unto her, 'Woman, believe me, the hour (time) cometh when ye shall neither in this mount nor yet at Jerusalem, worship the Father. Ye worship ye know not what. We know what we worship for salvation is of the Jews. But the hour (time) cameth, and now is when the true worshipper shall worship the Father in spirit and in truth for the Father seeketh such to worship him. God is a spirit, and they that worship him must worship him in spirit and in truth'" (John 4:20–24).

God created human beings to worship him, this is why we were created. Remember, worship is a relationship with God, this means you must be in covenant with God. Under the law of Moses, you were in covenant with God through circumcision of the flesh, which is a blood covenant, but now we are in covenant with God through the blood of Jesus, which is circumcision of the heart. The true worshipper must worship God in spirit and in truth. When we except Jesus as Savior and Lord, we receive the indwelling of the Holy Spirit, we cannot worship God in the flesh. "For we are the circumcision (pure in heart), which worship God in the Spirit and rejoice in Christ Jesus and have no confidence in the flesh" (Philippians 3:3). Jesus told the woman at the well that the time will come that she or we will neither worship in the mountain or Jerusalem, and what Jesus had said is true because the true worshippers, which is Christians, are worshipping the true and living God in churches all over the world. Christians are worshipping God every Sunday morning and in their life and lifestyle every day.

To be a son or daughter of God, you must have his Holy Spirit. We are all his creation, but we are not his sons and daughters, except we are born again by the blood of Jesus, which is a blood covenant between God and man. "For to be carnally (fleshly) minded is death, but to be spiritually minded is life and peace. Because the carnal mind is enmity against God for it is not subject to the law of God, neither indeed can be. So, then they that are in the flesh cannot please God. But ye are not in the flesh but in the Spirit, if so be that the Spirit of God dwell in you. Now if any man have not the Spirit of Christ, he is none of his" (Romans 8:6–9).

The world is led by the flesh, or the carnal minds, but the children of God are led by the Spirit of God. Yes, Christians have sinned from time to time because of the flesh, because in the flesh dwells no good things, because the flesh is sinful. Christians do not live in sin, sinners lives in sin. When a Christian sins, the Holy Spirit brings conviction to that Christian to repent of the that sin because you cannot serve God in sin or worship God in sin. "Now the works of the flesh are manifest, which are these: adultery, fornication, uncleanness, lasciviousness, idolatry, witchcraft, hatred, variance emulations, wrath, strife, seditions, heresies, envying, murders, drunkenness, reveling, and such like of the which I tell you before, as I have also told you in time past, that they which do such things shall not inherit the Kingdom of God. Christians do not live like this and say he is a Christian unless he is a carnal Christian and being led by the flesh rather than being led by the spirit. Sinners are led by the flesh because they are carnal and not saved. But Christians are saved and are led by the Holy Spirit. Remember, not good things dwelleth in the flesh, there is the works of the flesh and the fruit of the Spirit. But the fruit of the Spirit is love, joy, peace, long-suffering, gentleness, goodness, faith, meekness, temperance against such there is no law. And they that are Christ's have crucified the flesh with the affections and lusts. If we live in the Spirit, let us also walk in the Spirit. Let us not be desirous of vain glory, provoking one another" (Galatians 5:19–26).

Religious people serve and worship their god through the flesh, but Christians serve and worship the true and living God through the Holy Spirit because God is a Spirit, God is not flesh and blood. So, flesh and blood cannot worship the true and living God, we must worship God through the Holy Spirit. Only the true church, the body of believers can worship the true and living God. We all can praise God because he is worthy to be praised, because the Word of God said, "Let everything that hath breath praise the Lord. Praise ye the Lord" (Psalm 150:6).

Not only human being should praise the Lord, but all his creatures should praise the Lord. God cannot receive worship from religious people or sinners, only Christians. Are you a child of God or are you a child of Satan? Are you being led by the Holy Spirit? Or are you being led by the flesh? Is God your Father? Or Satan is your father? If you are born again, then God is your heavenly Father. If you are a sinner, then Satan is your father. There is no in between, either God is your Father or Satan is your father. There is only two fathers, God or Satan. There is only two kingdom, the kingdom of God and the kingdom of Satan. There is only two place you will go when you die, heaven or hell, the choice is yours. "Therefore, brethren, we are debtors, not to the flesh, to live after the flesh. For if you live after the flesh, ye shall die, but if ye through the Spirit, do mortify the deeds of the body, ye shall live. For as many as are led by the Spirit of God, they and the sons (children) of God. For ye have not received the Spirit of bondage again to fear, but ye have received the spirit of adoption, whereby we cry, Abba Father. The Spirit itself beareth witness with our spirit that we are the children of God" (Romans 8:12–16).

Jesus spoke these word to the Israelite, "This people draweth nigh unto me with their mouth and honoureth me with their lips, but their heart is far from me. But in vain they do worship me, teaching for doctrines the commandment of men" (Matthew 15:8–9). They worship God, but their worship was rejected because their hearts were corrupt with sin, their hearts were not pure, and their hearts were far from God. Only the pure in heart shall see God, and the only way to purify your hearts is by the blood of Jesus, not by

Judaism or any other religion or by the blood of bulls and goats but by the Lamb of God which takes away the sin of the world. Because worship is a relationship with God through Jesus. "'Ye are my witnesses,' saith the Lord, 'and my servant whom I have chosen that ye may know and believe me and understand that I am he. Before me, there was no God formed, neither shall there be after me. I, even I, am the Lord and beside me there is no savior. I have declared and have saved, and I have shown when there was no strange god among you; therefore, ye are my witnesses,' saith the Lord, 'that I am God. Yea, before the day was I am he, and there is none and who shall let it?' 'Thus,' saith the Lord, 'your redeemer, the Holy One of Israel'" (Isaiah 43:10–14).

"'Thus,' saith the Lord the King of Israel and his redeemer the Lord of hosts, 'I am the first and I am the last, and beside me there is no God. Fear ye not, neither be afraid, have not I told thee from that time and have declared it ye are even my witnesses. Is there a God beside me? Yea, there is no God, I know not any'" (Isaiah 44:6 and 8). There is only one God that can redeem, and his name is the Lord Jesus Christ. I would not serve a God that cannot redeem me. You have a lot of religion and a lot of religious leaders, and each one of these religion supposed to have a god, and if that is true, then where does these gods live, not in heaven because only the true and living reside in heaven, and he will not share his throne with anyone. "I am the Lord, that is my name, and my glory will I not give to another, neither my praise to graven images" (Isaiah 42:8). Remember, God is a Spirit, not graven images or flesh and blood. God was manifested in the flesh to redeemed us in the flesh. We worship God in the spirit, because we have his Holy Spirit that are Christian. We have God on a which is the Holy Spirit because we are his children that are born again.

"Then Paul stood in the midst of Mars Hill, and said, 'Ye, men of Athens, I perceive that in all things ye are too superstitious. For as I passed by and beheld your devotions (worship), I found and altar with this inscription, to the unknown god. Whom therefore ye ignorantly worship, him declare I unto you God that made the world and all things therein, seeing that he is Lord of heaven and earth, dwelleth not in temples made with hands, neither is worshipped with men's hands as though he needed anything, seeing he giveth to all life and breath and all things and hath made of one blood all nations of men for to dwell on all the face of the earth and hath determined the times before appointed and the bounds of their habitation. That they should seek the Lord, if haply they might feel after him and find him though he be not far from every one of us for in him we live and move and have our being as certain also of your own poets have said. For we are also his offspring. For as much then as we are the offspring of God, we ought not to think that the Godhead is like unto gold or silver or stone, graven by art and man's device. And the times of this ignorance God winked at but now commandeth all men everywhere to repent because he hath appointed a day, in the which he will judge the world in righteousness by that man whom he hath ordained, whereof he hath ordained, whereof he hath given assurance unto all men in that he hath raised him from the dead" (Acts 17:22–31).

If we were made in the image of God and we were, then we are not the offspring of graven images, we are not silver and gold, we are not stone, we are human being. Graven images cannot create the heavens and the earth; graven images cannot create human being or animals. Graven image cannot redeem or forgives sins, graven images cannot hear or answers prayers, graven images cannot hear, speak, or see, graven images are made by men. There is only one true and living God, there is only one true church, there is only one redeemer, and there is only one way to go to heaven, and that is through Jesus Christ, our Savior and Lord. "The law of the Lord is perfect converting the soul. The testimony of the Lord is sure, making wise the simple. The statutes of the Lord are right rejoicing the heart. The commandment of the Lord is pure, enlightening the eyes. More to be desired are they than gold, yea than much fine gold, sweeter also than honey and the honeycomb" (Psalm 19:7–10).

The Word of God is too pure and holy, the Word of God is perfect, the Word of God is too sure and too righteous to have been written by any men without the help of the Holy Spirit. The Word of God is God, the Word of God is inspired by God. God used men to write the Word of God by the inspiration of God. "All scripture is given by inspiration of God and is profitable for doctrine for reproof, for correction, for instruction in righteousness. That the man of God may be perfect, thoroughly furnished unto all good work" (2 Timothy 3:16–17). We have two days to establish to worship God. Under the law of Moses, we worshipped God on the Sabbath day which is Saturday, the seven day. Under the grace of the Lord Jesus Christ, we now worship God on Sunday because Jesus nailed the law of Moses to his cross and then was resurrected from the dead on Sunday, and fifty days later, the Holy Ghost came on Sunday. The Christian church was established to worship God on Sunday. All other religion worship on Saturday because if the other religion is on Sunday, they would have to accept the resurrection of Jesus Christ from the dead and that he is Lord and savior of the world. Remember, worship is a relationship with God through Jesus Christ, and Christians worship the true and living God on Sunday. This is why we worship God on Sunday, and if your religion does not worship God on Sunday, then you are not of the Christian faith and do not worship the true and living God. Satan always wanted you to worship him because he said, "I shall be like God." When the Lord Jesus Christ was led in the wilderness by the Spirit to be tempted by the devil, this was one of the temptations.

"And the devil, taking him up into an high mountain, showed unto him all the kingdoms of the world in a moment of time, and the devil said unto him, 'All this power will I give thee and the glory of them for that is delivered unto me and to whomsoever I will I give it. If thou therefore wilt worship me, all shall be thine.' And Jesus answered and said unto him, 'Get thee behind me, Satan, for it is written. Thou shalt worship the Lord thy God and him only shalt thou serve'" (Luke 4:5–8). If the devil would try to get Jesus to worship him, and Jesus Christ is God in the flesh, he will try to get you to worship him. The devil will give you popularity, fame, wealth, and stuff so you can serve him and worship him in exchange for your soul. "For we brought nothing into this world, and it is certain we can carry nothing out. And having food and raiment let us be therewith content" (1 Timothy 6:7–8).

What shall profit a man to gain the world, and lose his soul, or what shall a man give in exchange for his soul? Your soul is priceless, and your soul worth more than the whole world. Satan is trying to steal your soul through false religion and works of righteousness by telling you that your good works must outweigh your bad works. Works cannot wash away sins, only the blood of Jesus, and only God can forgive them through Jesus Christ our Lord and Savior. In the Old Testament, the Israelite some time worshipped idols, and when you worship idols, you are worshipping the devil and demons. The Israelites were worshiping the true and living God, but the devil keep pulling them away into idolatry. What is idolatry? Idolatry is to worship or give devotion to a physical object as a god or a false deity. Now Satan try to pull you away from God through false religion and false doctrines so that you will worship him. The Israelites worshipped idols because of the Gentile nations. They worshipped idols, and association brings in similarly. Christians should not have fellowship with the world unless they are being a witness to the world. "What say I then? That the idol is anything or that which is offered in sacrifice to idols is anything? But I say that the things which the Gentiles sacrifice, they sacrifice to devils and not to God, and I would not that ye should have fellowship with devils. Ye cannot drink the cup of the Lord and the cup of the devils. Ye cannot be partakers of the Lord's table and of the toddle of devils" (1 Corinthians 10:19–21).

Paul is talking about taking communion, the Lord's supper. You must be a Christian to take the Lord's supper because you must be in fellowship with God through Jesus Christ. Communion means communication or to fellowship. You cannot be in fellowship with God and in fellowship with the devil, you cannot be partaker of the Lord's table and the devil's table. You are either in fellowship with the Lord or in fellowship with the devil, there is no in between. Either Jesus Christ is your Lord or Satan is your lord. "To whom will ye liken me and make me equal and compare me, that we (Father, Son, Holy Ghost) may be like? They lavish gold out of bag and weigh silver in the balance and hire a goldsmith, and he maketh it a god. They fall down, yea, they worship. They bear him upon the shoulder.

They carry him and set him in his place, and he standeth. From his place shall he not remove. Yea, one shall cry unto him, yet can he not answer nor save him out of his trouble. Remember this, and show yourselves men, bring it again to mind, o ye transgressors. Remember the former things of old for I am God, and there is none else. I am God, and there is none like me. Declaring the end from the beginning and from ancient times the things that are not yet done, saying, 'My counsel (word) shall stand, and I will do all my pleasure'" (Isaiah 46:5–10).

Do not let the devil confuse you with all these false gods, these false religion, and false church. There is only one true and living God that can save, that can forgive sin, that can hear and answer prayer. There is only one true church, which worship the true and living God, which he purchase with his own blood on the cross, and there is only one savior of the world. Idols cannot save, idols or religion cannot forgive sin. Idols cannot hear or answer prayers. When Jesus Christ comes back for the true Christian church, then the seven-year tribulation will begin. At that time, you will either worship Satan and his images or be put to death. "And the rest of the men which were not killed by these plagues yet repented not of the works of their hands, that they should not worship devils and idols of gold and silver and brass and stone and of wood, which neither can see, nor hear, nor walk. Neither repented they of their murders, nor of their sorceries, nor of their fornication, nor of their thefts" (Revelation 9:20–21).

The battle is between God and Satan, and the battle is for your soul. Every time he steals a soul from God, Satan and those demands rejoice, and every time a soul gets saved, the angels in heaven rejoice. When a sinner dies in his sins, that's a soul for Satan. When sinners repent and becomes a Christian, that is one soul for God. We do not have to die lost because God had made away for us through Jesus Christ. You have a choice, follow God or follow Satan. "And he opened his mouth in blasphemy against God, to blaspheme his name and his tabernacle (church) and them that dwell in heaven. And it was given unto him to make war with the saints and to overcome them, and power was given him over all kindreds and tongues and nations. And all that dwell upon the earth shall worship him, whose names are not written in the book of life of the lamb slain from the foundation of the world" (Revelation 13:6–8).

"And he had power to give life unto the image of the beast, that the image of the beast should both speak and cause that as many as would not worship the image of the beast should be killed. And he causeth all, both small and great, rich and poor, free and bond, to receive a mark in their right hand or in their foreheads. And that no man might buy or sell, save he that had the mark or the name of the beast or the number of his name. Here is wisdom. Let him that hath understanding count the number of the beast for it is the number of a man, and his number is six hundred (600) threescore (60) and six (6) (666)" (Revelation 13:15–18).

Once you receive the mark of the beast in your forehead or right hand, you cannot change your mind when you rely that Jesus is the Christ, the savior of the world. Once you receive the mark of the beast, your soul belongs to Satan, and he will demand your worship. Remember, God created us to worship him, but Satan wants you to worship him. You cannot serve two master, either you will serve God or serve Satan, hate one or love the other, you are either in God's kingdom or in Satan's kingdom. To be in God's kingdom, you must be born again through Jesus Christ, our Lord and Savior. To be in Satan's kingdom, you just have to be an unbeliever and live like the devil. When it comes to righteousness, there is no middle ground, you are either saved or lost, righteous or unrighteous, justified or condemned. You are either on the Lord's side or you are on the devil's side. You are either on that old ship of Zion or that old, sinking ship of the devil. "And the third angel followed them, saying with a loud voice, 'If any man worship the beast and his image and receive his mark in his forehead or his hand, the same shall drink of the wine of the wrath of God, which is poured out without mixture into the cup of his indignation, and he shall be tormented with fire and brimstone in the presence of the holy angels and in the presence of the lamb. And the smoke of their torment ascendeth up forever and ever, and they have no rest day nor night who worship the beast and his images and whosoever receiveth the mark of his name" (Revelation 14:9–11).

Once you receive the mark of the beast, Satan becomes your lord and god. Satan will put pressure on you to receive the mark of the beast because you will not be able buy or sell without the mark of the beast. You will not be able to buy food, clothing, medicine, or anything with the mark in your forehead and right hand. But God is merciful that even through the seven-year tribulation, he makes a way for us to be saved through the everlasting gospel. "And I saw another angel fly in the midst of heaven, having the everlasting gospel to preach unto them that dwell on the earth and to every nation and kindred and tongue and people, saying with a loud voice, 'Fear God and give glory to him for the hour of his judgment is come and worship him that made heaven and earth and the sea and the fountains of waters'" (Revelation 14:6–7).

The holy angels preached the everlasting gospel to those that are left behind to be saved, they did not preach the doctrine of water baptism. To the outmost Jesus saves. They did not preach the doctrine of speaking in tongue, they preached the everlasting gospel. The gospel is everlasting because the gospel is Jesus Christ. "From everlasting to everlasting, thou art God." Without believing the gospel of Jesus Christ, you cannot be saved. Then you are baptized, the Holy Ghost baptism.

# Jesus Is Our Resurrection and Our Life

Without the Lord Jesus Christ, we could not get up because Jesus Christ is God in the flesh. Only the true and living God have the power to raise the dead. If your god do not have the power to raise the dead, then maybe he is not God because there is nothing too hard for the true and living God, he even have power over death. "Then said Martha unto Jesus, 'Lord, if thou hast been here, my brother had not died. But I know, that even now, whatsoever thou wilt ask of God, God will give it thee.' Jesus saith unto her, 'Thy brother shall rise again.' Martha saith unto him, 'I know that he shall rise again in the resurrection at the last day.' Jesus said unto her, 'I am the resurrection and the life. He that believeth in me though he were dead yet shall he live. And whosoever liveth and believeth in me shall never die. Believeth thou this?' She saith unto him, 'Yea, Lord. I believe that thou art the Christ, the Son of God, which should come into the world'" (John 11:21–27).

Martha was a Christian, and she believed in the resurrection, so she knew that her brother, Lazarus, shall live again at the resurrection, but Jesus wanted her to know that he has the power to raise Lazarus from the dead now because he is the resurrection and the life. Without Jesus nobody can be resurrected because he gives to all eternal life that believes in him, or to those who do not believe the gospel of the Lord Jesus Christ, they shall receive eternal damnation. "Verily, Verily, I say unto you, he that heareth my word and believeth on him that sent me hath everlasting life and shall not come into condemnation but is passed from death unto life. Verily, Verily, I say unto you, the hour is coming, and now is, when the dead shall hear the voice of the Son of God, and they that hear shall live. For as the Father hath life in himself so hath he given to the son to have life in himself and hath given him authority to execute judgment also because he is the son of man. Marvel not at this for the hour is coming, in the which all that are in the graves shall hear is voice and shall come forth. They that have done good unto the resurrection of life, and they that have done evil unto the resurrection of damnation" (John 5:24–29).

There is two resurrection, the resurrection of the saved dead, those that died in the Lord Jesus Christ by believing the gospel of Jesus Christ, and the resurrection of the lost dead, those that died in their sins and in cults and false religions. The saved dead will be resurrected at the return of Christ's coming. Then the seven-year tribulation, the battle of Armageddon, and the millennial reign of the Lord Jesus Christ. And then the resurrection of the lost dead and then the great white throne judgment of the lost dead. "But I would not have you to be ignorant, brethren, concerning them which are asleep (dead), that ye sorrow not even as others which have no hope. For if we believe that Jesus died and rose again, even so them also which sleep (died) in Jesus will God bring with him. For this we say unto you by the word of the Lord that we which are alive and remain unto the coming of the Lord shall not prevent them which are asleep (dead). For the Lord himself shall descend from heaven with a shout, with the voice of the archangel, and with the trump of God, and the dead in Christ shall rise first. Then we which are alive and remain shall be caught up together with them in the clouds to meet the Lord in the air and so shall we ever be with the Lord. Wherefore comfort one another with these words" (1 Thessalonians 4:13–18).

When a Christian dies in Jesus Christ, we have hope in God that we shall live again and be with the Lord in heaven, but when a sinner dies, he dies without any hope at all, he dies lost and eternally damn. The devil wants to damn your soul into hell, that is why he attacks the gospel of Jesus Christ. The devil attacks the death of Jesus, the devil attacks the burial of Jesus, the devil attacks the resurrection of Jesus, which is the gospel of Jesus Christ. The devil tries to make you doubt the virgin birth of Jesus, the devil tries to make you doubt the death of Jesus on the cross to atone for our sins, he tries to make you doubt the burial and resurrection of Jesus for your justification.

Without the gospel of Jesus Christ, there is no Christianity and there is no resurrection. Why would the apostle preach about a dead savior? Or why would they give their life for a dead Savior? For the gospel of Jesus Christ. The apostles gave their lives for the gospel because Jesus is alive and well. He is seated on the right hand side of God in heaven, with all power in heaven and on earth, and he will come back for the true church someday, the body of believers in Christ Jesus. "But some man will say, 'How are the dead raised up? And with what body do they come?'" (1 Corinthians 15:35).

"So also is the resurrection of the dead. It is sown in corruption, it is raised in incorruption, is sown in dishonor, it is raised in glory, it is sown in weakness, it is raised in power: It is a natural body, it is raised a spiritual body. There is a natural body, and there is a spiritual body. And so it is written, the first man Adam was made a living soul, the last Adam (Christ) was made a quickening spirit" (1 Corinthians 15:42–45). Remember we are flesh, spirit, and soul. The flesh goes back to the ground where it came from, but the spirit and the soul return back to God where it came from if you die as a Christian. But if you die as a sinner, or some other religion, your spirit and soul belong to the devil in hell. Either Jesus is your Lord or Satan is your lord. You cannot serve two masters, you will love one and hate the other. The devil will tell you that there is no resurrection of the dead and that you are reincarnated, rebirth of the soul in a new body, but that is a lie from the devil and the pit of hell. You will live again and stand before God as your judge or savior. "Now this I say, brethren, that flesh and blood cannot inherit the Kingdom of God, neither doth corruption inherit incorruption. Behold, I show you a mystery. We shall not all sleep (die), but we shall all be changed, in a moment, in the twinkling of an eye, at the last trump for the trumpet shall sound, and the dead shall be raised incorruptible, and we shall be changed. For this corruptible must put on incorruption, and this mortal must put on immortality" (1 Corinthians 15:50–53).

Our flesh and blood cannot go to heaven because our flesh is corrupted with sin because no good thing dwells in the flesh. Our blood is tainted with sin which we inherit through the bloodline of the first Adam. To go to heaven, you must be born again, your sin is forgiven by God, and washed by the blood of Jesus Christ and be regenerated by the Holy Ghost. "So when this corruptible shall have put on incorruption and this mortal shall have put on immortality, then shall be brought to pass the saying that is written, 'Death is swallowed up in victory.' O death, where is thy sting? O grave, where is thy victory? The sting of death is sin, and the strength of sin is the law. But thank be to God which giveth us the victory through our Lord Jesus Christ. Therefore, my beloved brethren, be ye steadfast, unmovable, always abounding in the work of the Lord for as much as ye know that you labor is not in vain in the Lord" (1 Corinthians 15:54–58).

God have given us the victory over the sting of death, hell, and the grave through Jesus Christ our Lord and Savior because Jesus have tokened the sting out of death. Christians does not receive the sting of death because we have died in the Lord Jesus Christ. When sinners die, they receive the sting of death because they have died in their sins. When a Christian die, he just falls asleep, but when a sinner die, he is dead because the ages of sin is death, but the gift of God is eternal life through Jesus Christ our Lord. Religion cannot save you, only Jesus can save; religion cannot forgive your sins, only God through Jesus Christ. "And on highway shall be there, and a way, and it shall be called the way of holiness. The unclean shall not pass over it, but it shall be for those the way faring men, though fools, shall not err therein" (Isaiah 35:8).

"Fellow peace with all men and holiness, without which no man shall see the Lord" (Hebrews 12:14). Jesus is our holiness because he bore our sin in his body on the cross, and our sins are cleansed by his blood. Religion cannot make you holy. Religion cannot forgive your sins because someone has to atone for your sins. There is only one true religion, Christianity, all other religion will fail you.

# Jesus Bear Our Judgment

After the resurrection of the church, the body of believer, the seven-year tribulation will begin, and after the seven-year tribulation, the battle of Armageddon will begin, and after the battle of Armageddon, the millennial reign will begin. The saints will reign with Jesus for a thousand years in his millennial kingdom on earth. Then will be the great white throne judgment. "It is a faithful saying, for if we be dead with him, we shall also live with him. If we suffer, we shall also reign with him. If we deny him, he also will deny us. If we believe not, yet he abideth faithful, he cannot deny himself" (2 Timothy 2:11–13).

During the seven-year tribulation, the wrath of God will be poured out. You will not be able to buy or sell without the mark of the beast in your forehead and on your right hand; the mark of the beast is 666. The wrath of God began by opening the seven seals, which begin in the six chapter. Then when the seventh seal is open, then the wrath of God is unleash again by the blowing of the seven trumpets, which begin in the eighth chapter of revelation. Then the wrath of God through the seven vials, which began in the fifteenth chapter of revelation. But God is so merciful that you still can be saved doing the seven-year tribulation. "And the beast was taken and with him the false prophet that wrought miracles before him, with which he deceived them that had received the mark of the beast and them that worshipped his image. These both were cast alive into a lake of fire burning with brimstone" (Revelation 19:20). "And the devil that deceived them was cast into the lake of fire and brimstone, where the beast and the false prophet are and shall be tormented day and night forever and ever" (Revelation 20:10).

We see that the false prophet received judgment and the beast (anti-Christ) received judgment and the devil received judgment, the unholy trinity, and they all were cast into the lake of fire and brimstone. And all sinners that died lost will stand before the great white throne to be judged. And about the ninth hour, Jesus cried with a loud voice, saying, "*Eli, Eli, lama sabachthani?*" That is to say, "My God, my God, why hast thou forsaken me" because God "Hath made him to be sin for us, who knew no sin that we might be made the righteousness of God in him" (2 Corinthians 5:21). Jesus bear our sins on the cross, and then God judged him, so Jesus bear our judgment so we do not have to be judged. The righteousness will not be judged, only the unrighteous, self-righteous, sinners, and the religious. Christians will not be judged because we have accepted Jesus Christ as Savior and Lord. "And as it is appointed unto men once to die but after this the judgment, so Christ was once offered to bear the sin of many and unto them that look for him shall he appear the second time without sin unto salvation" (Hebrews 9:27–28).

"And I saw a great white throne and him that sat on it, from whose face the earth and the heaven fled away, and there was found no place for them. And I saw the dead, small and great, stand before God, and the books were opened, and another book was opened which is the book of life. And the dead were judged out of those things which were written in the book, according to their works. And the sea gave up the dead which were in it, and death and hell delivered up the dead which were in them, and they were judged every man according to their works. And death and hell were cast into the lake of fire. This is the second death. And whosoever was not found written in the book of life was cast into the lake of fire" (Revelation 20:11–15).

God is a holy God, he is a righteous God, he is a just God, and God must judge sin. Jesus Christ is the sin bearer for the whole world. Jesus was judged by God on the cross so we would not be judged, if we received him as Savior and Lord. If you die in your sin, you will be judged and cast into the lake of fire, which is the second death. Those that died in Jesus Christ will inherit eternal life. Christians will not stand before the judgment throne of God, Christians will stand before the judgment seat of Christ to receive our reward. "For we must all appear before the judgment seat of Christ that every one may receive the things done in his body according to that he hath done, whether it be good or bad" (2 Corinthians 5:10) Hell is real, it is more than just a grave. The word *Sheol* means the grave; the word *Gehenna* means a trash dump, but the word *Hades* means a literal hell, which burns with fire and brimstone, forever and forever. The word Sheol is used as a metaphor, the grave or Jonah in the belly of the whale. "And said, 'I cried by reason of mine affliction unto the Lord, and he heard me out of the belly of hell cried I, and thou heardest my voice'" (Jonah 2:2)

This is a metaphor, Sheol but Jesus is talking about a real hell which burn with fire and brimstone. "Then shall he say also unto them on the left hand, 'Depart from me, ye cured, into everlasting fire (hell), prepared for the devil and his angels'" (Matthew 25:41). Hell were not made for humans, we were created to worship and follow God, not Satan. Hell were made for the devil and his angels. We believe that all children dying in infancy, having not actually transgressed against the law of God, in their own persons are only subject to the first death, which was brought down by the fall of the first Adam, and not that any one of them dying in that state shall suffer punishment in hell by guilt of Adam's sin for of such is the kingdom of God. Animals cannot and will not be judged by God because animals do not possess a soul, only human beings possess a soul. The soul is the will, mind, and emotion of a human being. We have a free will to worship and serve God or reject him and serve Satan. The animals that is talked about in the book of Isaiah the prophet is in the millennia kingdom, the thousand-year reign of Christ here on earth.

"And righteousness shall be the girdle of his loins and faithfulness the girdle of his reins. The wolf also shall dwell with the lamb, and the leopard shall lie down with the kid, and the calf and the young lion and the fatling together, and a little child shall lead them. And the cow and the bear shall feed, their young ones shall lie down together. And the lion shall eat straw like the ox. And the sucking child shall play on the hole of the asp, and the weaned child shall put his hand on the cockatrice den" (Isaiah 11:5–8).

The Lord Jesus Christ shall reign in his kingdom for one thousand years, and the church, the bride of Christ, shall reign with him. For if we suffer with him, we shall also reign with him. And doing the time of the reign of Jesus Christ in this millennial kingdom for a thousand years, Satan will be cast in the bottomless pit for a thousand years. "And I saw an angel come down from heaven, having the key of the bottomless pit and great chain in his hand. And he laid hold on the dragon, that old serpent, which is the devil, and Satan and bound him a thousand years and cast him into the bottomless pit and shut him up and set a seal upon him, that he should deceive the nations no more till the thousand years should be fulfilled, and after that, he must be loosed a little season" (Revelation 20:1–3).

After the thousand-year reign of Jesus Christ, the Lord Jesus Christ will judge the whole world, all nations, kindreds, and tongues. Jesus Christ will either be your savior or your judge. Jesus is the savior of the world, and you must be saved, born again to go to heaven. "And I saw thrones and they sat upon them, and judgment was given unto them, and I saw the souls of them that were beheaded for the witness of Jesus and for the Word of God and which had not worshipped the beast, neither his image, neither had received his mark upon their foreheads, or in their hands, and they lived and reigned with Christ a thousand years. But the rest of the dead lived not again until the thousand years were finished. This is the first resurrection. Blessed and holy is he that hath part in the first resurrection on such the second death hath no power, but they shall be priests of God and of Christ and shall reign with him a thousand years" (Revelation 20:4–6).

The tribulation believer were beheaded because they refuse to worshipped the beast and his image and refuse the mark of the beast, 666. There is a first and second coming of Jesus Christ. The first time Jesus came, he came as savior of the world and made atonement for the sins of the world. The second time he comes, he will come for his bride, the church, the body of believers in Jesus Christ. There is two resurrection, the first resurrection is the resurrection of the church, the saved dead, those that died in the Lord Jesus Christ. The second resurrection is the lost dead, those that died as a sinner or religious, self-righteous. The second death is eternal damnation or eternal death into the lake of fire. So, make your choice, eternal death or eternal life, which is through our Lord and Savior, Jesus Christ.

"And when the thousand years are expired, Satan shall be loosed out of his prison and shall go out to deceive the nations which are in the four quarters of the earth, Gog and Magog, to gather them together to battle, the number of whom is as the sand of the sea. And they went up on the breadth of the earth and compassed the camp of the saints about and the beloved city, and fire came down from God out of heaven and devoured them" (Revelation 20:7–9). It is finish, Satan is defeated, Jesus is King of king and Lord of lords, and everyone received their just reward. The false prophet and the beast are cast into the lake of fire, Satan is cast into the lake of fire, and the wicket dead are cast into the lake of fire, which burn with fire and brimstone forever and forever. The righteous and saved dead shall receive their reward from God.

We shall receive the crown of righteous. "For I am now ready to be offered, and the time of my departure is at hand. I have fought a good fight, I have finish my course, I have kept the faith. Henceforth there is laid up for me a crown of righteousness, which the Lord, the righteous judge, shall give me at that day, and not to me only but unto all them also that love his appearing" (2 Timothy 4:6–8). We shall receive the crown of life. "Blessed is the man that endureth temptation for when he is tried, he shall receive the crown of life, which the Lord hath promised to them that love him" (James 1:12). We shall receive the crown of glory. "And when the chief shepherd shall appear, ye shall receive a crown of a glory that fadeth not away" (1 Peter 5:4).

We shall receive the crown of joy. "For what is our hope or joy or crown of rejoicing? Are not even ye in the presence of our Lord Jesus Christ at his coming?" (1 Thessalonians 2:19) We shall receive an incorruptible crown. "And every man that striveth for the mastery is temperate in all things. Now they do it to obtain a corruptible crown but we an incorruptible" (1 Corinthians 9:25). "Fear none of those things which thou shalt suffer. Behold, the devil shall cast some of you into prison that ye may be tried, and ye shall have tribulation ten days, be thou faithful unto death, and I will give thee a crown of life" (Revelation 2:10). These are the crown of the Christians, which faded not away. The glories of man and everything man do will fade away, only what you do for God will last.

Man have tried to play God by cloning, but man cannot clone a human being because man cannot clone a spirit, and man cannot clone a soul because the spirit and soul come from God and the flesh come from the dust of the earth. Man is body, spirit, and soul. The body return back to the ground, the spirit must be quickened, and the soul will be judged; only your soul can be saved. Flesh and blood cannot be saved, neither can flesh and blood inherit the kingdom of God. "The Lord is not slack concerning his promise as some men count slackness but is long-suffering to us-ward, not willing that any should perish but that all should come to repentance. But the day of the Lord will come as a thief in the night, in the which the heaven shall pass away with a great noise, and the elements shall melt with fervent heat, the earth also and the works that are therein shall be burned up. Seeing then that all these things shall be dissolved, what manner of persons ought ye to be in all holy conversation (lifestyle) and godliness, looking for and hasting unto the coming of the day of God, wherein the heavens being on fire shall be dissolved and the elements shall melt with fervent heat? Nevertheless, we, according to his promise, look for new heavens and a new earth, wherein dwelleth righteousness." (2 Peter 3:9–13). We will have a new heaven and a new earth because God will purge the heavens and the earth with fire because of sin. "Bless are the meek for they shall inherit the earth" (Matthew 5:5).

"And I saw a new heaven and a new earth for the first heaven and the first earth were passed away, and there was no more sea. And I, John, saw the holy city, new Jerusalem coming down from God out of heaven, prepared as a bride adorned for her husband. And I heard a great voice out of heaven saying, 'Behold, the tabernacle of God is with men, and he will dwell with them, and they shall be his people, and God himself shall be with them and be their God. And God shall wipe away all tears from their eyes, and there shall be no more death, neither sorrow nor crying, neither shall there be any more pain for the former things are passed away'" (Revelation 21:1–4). Not only the true believer in Jesus Christ have received their golden crowns, but the true church, the bride of Jesus Christ, the kingdom of God, have inherited the kingdom of heaven, and we shall be with the Lord forever and forever. This is the reward of the believers in Christ Jesus. "And he said unto me, 'It is done. I am alpha and omega, the beginning and the end. I will give unto him that is athirst of the fountain of the water of life freely. He that overcometh shall inherit all things, and I will be his God, and he shall be my son. But the fearful and the unbelieving and the abominable and murderers and whoremongers and sorcerers and idolaters and all liars shall have their part in the lake which burneth with fire and brimstone, which is the second death'" (Revelation 21:6–8).

And this is the reward of the wicket dead who follow Satan and his ways. There are two kingdoms, one will go to heaven and one will go to hell. There is two ship, the Lord's ship, which is that old ship of Zion, and the devil's ship, which is a sinking ship. The church of the true and living God wins, and the churches of Satan loses. "The four and twenty elders fall down before him that sat on the throne and worship him that liveth forever and ever and cast their crowns before the throne, saying, 'Thou art worthy, o Lord, to receive glory and honor and power for thou hast created all things and for thy pleasure they are and were created'" (Revelation 4:10–11).

The twenty-four elders bow down and worshipped the true and living God. These elders represent the church because the church was created to worship God because he is worthy of our praise and worship. "And he carried me away in the spirit to a great and high mountain and showed me that great city, the holy Jerusalem, descending out of heaven from God, having the glory of God, and her light was like unto a stone most precious, even like a jasper stone, clear as crystal, and had a wall great and high and had twelve gates and names written thereon, which are the names of the twelve tribes of the children of Israel. On the east three gates, on the north three gates, on the south three gates, and on the west three gates. And the wall of the city had twelve foundations and in them the names of the twelve apostles of the lamb" (Revelation 21:10–14).

The names of the twelve elders of the twelve tribes of Israel on the twelve gates of the holy city represent the Old Testament church, and the names of the twelve apostles on the twelve foundation of the holy city represent the New Testament church. And the Word of God is the foundation of the church and the foundation of the holy city, which the prophets of the Old Testament and the apostles of the New Testament preached. "And behold, I come quickly, and my reward is with me to give every man according as his work shall be. I am alpha and omega, the beginning and the end, the first and the last. Blessed are they that do his commandments that they may have right to the tree of life and may enter in through the gates into the city. For without are dogs and sorcerers and whoremongers and murderers and idolaters and whatsoever loveth and maketh a lie. I, Jesus, have sent mine angel (preachers) to testify unto you these things in the churches. I am the root and the offspring of David and the bright and morning star" (Revelation 22:12–16).

Endure hardness as a good soldier of Jesus Christ, endure trials and tribulations, persecutions and afflictions, and run this race with patience because the church wins. God is holy, just and merciful, the creator, preserver and governor of the universe, the redeemer, savior, sanctifier and judge of men, and the only proper object of worship. The mode of his existence, however, is a subject far above the understanding of men, finite beings cannot comprehend him. There is nothing in the universe that can justly represent him for there is none like him; he is the fountain of all perfection and holiness and happiness. He is glorified by the whole creation and is worthy to be love and worshipped and served by all intelligence.

"Now unto him that is able to keep you from falling and to present you faultless before the presence of his glory with exceeding joy, to the only wise God, our Savior, be glory and majesty, dominion and power, both now and ever. Amen" (Jude 1:24–25).

# About the Author

Charles Holmes Sr. was born in Georgetown, South Carolina. He was a high school graduate of Howard High School. He also joined the United States Marine Corps in 1980. Later on, he graduated boot camp in Parris Island, which led to his first duty station being in Okinawa, Japan, third marine division; Camp Pendleton, California, first marine division; and Camp Lejeune, North Carolina, second marine division. He has two honorable discharges (August 1991) as a sergeant. Charles participated in Operation Desert Shield/Operation Desert Storm. He accepted his calling in the Lord Jesus Christ in February 17, 1997. He has been the pastor of Sandhill and Wilson Grove United American Free Will Baptist Church. He is the first vice bishop of the United American Free Will Baptist conference in South Carolina. He is married to Lucille Holmes for thirty-four years from January 21, 1986, to the present day. He is a father of two children, Charles Holmes Jr. and Charleshia Holmes. He also worked for Domino's for twenty-one years. He was inspired by the Holy Ghost Spirit and his Lord and Savior Jesus Christ to write this book.